ACTIVATING
WHAT'S *in* YOUR
BORN-AGAIN
SPIRIT

ACTIVATING
WHAT'S *in* YOUR
BORN-AGAIN
SPIRIT

4 Steps to Activate
What You've Already Got!

DR. LON STETTLER

XULON PRESS

Xulon Press
2301 Lucien Way #415
Maitland, FL 32751
407.339.4217
www.xulonpress.com

Unless otherwise indicated, Scripture quotations taken from the New American Standard Bible (NASB). Copyright © 1960, 1962, 1963, 1968, 1971, 1972, 1973, 1975, 1977, 1995 by The Lockman Foundation. Used by permission. All rights reserved.

Scripture quotations taken from the New King James Version (NKJV). Copyright © 1982 by Thomas Nelson, Inc. Used by permission. All rights reserved.

Printed in the United States of America.

ISBN-13: 978-1-6312-9166-1

Endorsements

I highly recommend Dr. Lon Stettler's book as a roadmap to a deeper spiritual life. This book gave me a deeper realization of who I am in Christ. I was challenged to respond in faith to what God has already provided. By understanding Dr. Stettler's teaching on who you are in Christ and the truth about your born-again spirit, you will revitalize your desire to live for Him. The practical aspect of Dr. Stettler's four-step activation process will help your faith come alive, resulting in you becoming "doers of the word and not hearers only." Finally, getting rid of the false identities that you have and putting on the true identity you have in Christ will become clearer as you go through the meditations at the end of the book.

Ronald Ovitt, Author, teacher, and president of Empower Ministry, Chicago, Illinois

Dr. Lon Stettler's spiritual gift is teaching which will become very evident as you read this book. He lays out the principles of body, soul, and spirit and how they work together in the life of the believer in a very clear and practical way. He lays a solid foundation, filled with scripture and application, describing who we are in Jesus Christ and the power of God's grace. The thirty-three-day activation devotional is powerful and will help any believer "grow in the grace and knowledge of our Lord and Savior Jesus Christ" (2 Peter 3:18).

Larry Burgbacher, Lead Pastor, Faith Church, Summerville, South Carolina

I have known Dr. Lon Stettler for over thirty years. When I tell you that he is a student of the Word, that is a gross understatement. His insight in helping the reader discover who they are in Christ is refreshing and invigorating. The most foundational principles in following Christ include the discoveries that we are loved, chosen, accepted, adopted, secure, and significant. Do yourself a favor and dive into this book with an open heart and mind. You won't regret it.

Brad Rosenberg, Lead Pastor, Tri-County Assembly of God, Cincinnati, Ohio

I have enjoyed getting to know Lon Stettler and hearing his heart and teaching over the past couple of years here at Faith Church. There are so many roadblocks in discovering your true identity in Christ. *Activating What's in Your Born-Again Spirit* shows us the perspective shift that every believer needs to experience on what it truly means to be loved by your Creator. I love the thirty-three practical activating points and prayers that literally lift and rid the spirit of condemnation and awaken our born-again spirit! As you read this book, you will discover what the Bible really says about who you are in Christ and the practical ways to live and initiate a life of faith.

Jason Burgbacher, Executive Pastor, Faith Church, Summerville, South Carolina

This book is a must-read for both the new and seasoned believer. Dr. Stettler states what the new believer needs to know as they begin their personal journey with Christ. He explains how God sees and values them and how they are deeply loved. He goes into detail on how they can activate what God has already given them in their born-again spirit so they can activate the gifts they have been blessed with. It also lightens the path for believers who already have a relationship with Christ—with "missed" Godly knowledge that will open their eyes to new understanding that could have been missed for many years. Everyone should read this book at least once and consider adding it to their yearly reading plan.

Lisa Carreiro, Project Management Professional, Summerville, South Carolina

Lon Stettler guides readers through a fascinating process of advancing their love relationship with God, our heavenly Father. The explanation of the interactions shared between the body, soul, and spirit revolutionized my spiritual walk. This book is simply a masterpiece as it blissfully and purposely moves readers to see themselves as God our heavenly Father sees them — deeply loved, completely forgiven and highly valued!

Dr. Patricia A. Ferguson, Career Planning Manager, Charleston, South Carolina

Table of Contents

Dedication

This book is dedicated first to my Lord Jesus Christ, who through the ministry of the Holy Spirit, opened my eyes to my real identity in Christ. This revelation of my identity and how to activate that identity has truly revolutionized both how I view the Lord and view myself. What a liberating and victorious way to live!

This book is also dedicated to my wonderful wife, Laurie, my companion, confidant, and friend. Her support and encouragement has been invaluable in the writing of this book. Laurie graciously co-labors with me in the work of the ministry.

Foreword

I still remember it like it was yesterday, the day that I was first introduced to the process of *Activation.* I didn't know that was what it was called or what it really meant. It was much later before I realized that the process of activation is how the kingdom of God works.

It was one Sunday morning in August, and the worship service at the church I was attending to qualify to play on the church's softball team had just concluded. I had played softball for the church for two seasons and really felt at home at this church. The pastor, Roger, played on the softball team as well, and I had gotten to know him fairly well. I told him that I really liked the church and wanted to become a member. I wanted to belong and find my purpose.

Roger invited me to join him in the pastor's office. He pulled out a Bible and opened to a passage that I have gotten to know quite well:

> *The word is near you, in your mouth and in your heart—that is the word of faith which we are preaching, that if you confess with your mouth Jesus as Lord, and believe in your heart that God raised Him from the dead, you will be saved; for with the heart a person believes, resulting in righteousness, and with the mouth he confesses, resulting in salvation . . . faith comes from hearing, and hearing by the word of Christ. (*Rom. 10:8–10, 17)

He talked me through the passage and asked if I had any questions. I asked a couple of clarifying questions that he answered. Then, Roger stepped away and asked that I continue to review these verses. Unbeknownst to me, he stepped out of his office and joined his wife and they began to pray that I would receive Christ as my Savior that day.

When Roger returned, he led me through the four steps of activation. I heard the *Word* that Roger spoke, and I believed in my heart that Jesus was Lord and that God raised Him from the dead. He then led me to confess with my mouth that Jesus is Lord and to repent of my sins, asking God to forgive me of all my sins. I then invited Jesus Christ into my heart to be my Savior and Lord. At that point, I felt an assurance that I was now a child of God—a result of salvation. That day I experienced the first application of the activation process in life.

This book is about the next application of the activation process: activating what has transpired in my born-again spirit and making it operational in my soul—my mind and heart. This process has been so revolutionary for me, helping me to develop a righteousness consciousness and understanding of who I am on the inside. What a liberating way to live!

As you read through this book, I trust that the activation process will be revolutionary for you as well.

Dr. Lon Stettler
Charleston, South Carolina

Introduction

For we are His workmanship [masterpiece], *created in Christ Jesus.*
(Eph. 2:10a, bracket added)

I t has been said that *art*—such as music, a sculpture, a painting—represents the *artist*. If you want to know an artist, simply study their work, and you will gain understanding of the artist.

God is the ultimate and greatest of all artists. The crowning jewel of God's creation is you. You are His masterpiece. This is what we will be learning in this book—learning about the art you are and the Artist, God.

If you want to see the *best-of-the-best* of all God has made in the universe, you don't need a telescope or a microscope. What you need is a mirror—more specifically, a *spiritual mirror!*[1,3]

The Scripture—God's Word—is our spiritual mirror. Let's begin to see God's perspective. The first step is to look closely in God's mirror.

In the first chapter of the book of James, the writer makes reference to two different mirrors. In verse 23, James refers to a physical mirror like the bathroom mirror you probably looked into this morning:

> *For if anyone is a hearer of the word and not a doer, he is like a man who looks at his natural face in a* **mirror**.

Then in verse 25, he refers to a *spiritual* mirror, which is God's Word:

> *But one who looks intently at the perfect law, the law of liberty* [God's Word— specifically the New Testament], *and abides by it, not having become a forgetful hearer but an effectual doer, this man will be blessed in what he does.*

Now, God's Word as a spiritual mirror addresses every facet of our lives, but for our purpose God's Word *perfectly* reflects who you are in your born-again spirit. "Therefore if anyone is in Christ, he is a new creature, the old things passed away; behold, new things have come" (2 Cor. 5:17). God's Word as a spiritual mirror is reflecting perfectly who you are in your born-again spirit.

Have you ever read God's Word, specifically the New Testament, and wondered if the writer is talking about your born-again spirit or your soul? I have. Then, I started asking the Holy Spirit, who moved upon men to write the Scriptures, to help me discern whether the author was speaking about my born-again spirit or my soul. It made all the difference in the world!

I remember a small group leader asking me, "Are you holy?" and "Are you righteous?" At that time, I respond something like, "I try to live a holy life." or "I try to be righteous." Over time, I learned that I lacked understanding of the relationship between my spirit and soul. I seemed to mesh the two together. I was mixing up what Christ did and what I do. I now know that I am holy and righteous in my born-again spirit as a result of the finished work of Christ. My responsibility now is to live out what has already transpired in my born-again spirit—live out holiness.

The *first section* of this book is about discerning the difference between soul and spirit, and it focuses on what is true about your born-again spirit. As you read God's Word about your born-again spirit, your task is to trust the spiritual reality you see in the Word.

As we begin, I invite you to reach for your Bible and hold it in your hands and make this declaration with me, often used by Pastor Joel Osteen of Lakewood Church in his broadcasts:

> "This is my Bible. I am who it says *I am*. I have what it says *I have*. And I *can do* what it says I can do."

Your born-again spirit accurately reflects who you *are*, what you *have* in Christ, and what you *can do* through Him.

Let's look into the spiritual mirror again with another verse in the New Testament that refers to a *spiritual mirror.*

> *But we all, with unveiled face, beholding as in a mirror* [God's Word] *the glory of the Lord* [reflecting the glory of your born-again spirit]*, are being transformed*

[in your soul] *into the same image* [found in your born-again spirit] *from glory to glory.* (2 Cor. 3:18) (brackets mine)

Notice this verse is *not* speaking of our born-again spirit that is being transformed, as our spirit being was completely transformed when we were born again. Rather, this verse is talking about our *soul* that is being transformed.

As you gaze into God's spiritual mirror, His Word, your soul begins to see with spiritual eyes and become transformed to what is in your born-again spirit. Your soul needs to catch up with what has already transpired in your born-again spirit. Your soul is what is being transformed.

> Your soul needs to catch up with what has already transpired in your born-again spirit.

Paul said to the Galatians:

My little children [Galatian believers], *with whom I am again in labor until Christ* [in your born-again spirit] *is formed in you* [your soul and heart]. (Gal. 4:19, brackets mine)

Likewise, Paul said to the Philippians:

Work out [activate into your soul] *your salvation* [from your born-again spirit] *with fear and trembling.* (Phil. 2:12, brackets mine)

Paul was saying that what is true about your born-again spirit does *not* automatically become active and operational in your soul; these truths must be implanted or activated. He labored with the Galatians, the Philippians, and all the churches to activate the believers' identity in Christ so their souls would catch up to their born-again spirit. The process of activation must be intentional and deliberate on the part of the believer.

> What is true about your born-again spirit does *not* automatically become active and operational in your soul; these truths must be implanted or activated.

The *second section* of this book will then show you how to activate your soul and into your life what has already transpired in your born-again spirit.

The *third section* brings the two together—apply the activation process to each truth about your born-again spirit.

Let's first learn about the real you that God created you to be in your born-again spirit, and then how your soul becomes transformed.

SECTION 1

Discerning Soul and Spirit

For the word of God is living and active and sharper than any two-edged sword,
and piercing as far as the division of <u>soul</u> *and* <u>spirit,</u> *of both joints and marrow,*
and able to judge the thoughts and intentions of the heart.
(Heb. 4:12, underline added)

The writer of the book of Hebrews and the apostle Paul clearly understood the distinction between soul and spirit. Paul told the Thessalonian believers, "may your *spirit,* and *soul* and body be preserved complete, without blame at the coming of our Lord Jesus Christ" (1 Thess. 5:23).

To a great extent, the Christian life consists of your soul catching up with what has already transpired in your born-again spirit as you move toward full personhood—from glory to glory. Your mind and heart are being "transformed by the renewing your mind" (Rom. 12:2). As a result of implanting the word in your soul, your soul becomes conformed to your God-image—the image of Christ (Rom. 8:29). The end goal of the activation process is to move you from a sin-consciousness view of yourself *to developing the gold standard, a righteousness consciousness'.*

Chapter 1

Jesus in the Mirror

You were created to look and be like God. The psalmist said you are "fearfully and wonderfully made."

> *Then God said, "Let Us make man in Our image, according to our likeness . . . God created man in His own image.* (Gen. 1:26–27)

> *. . . I am fearfully* [to stand in awe of] *and wonderfully made.* (Psalm 139:14b, brackets mine)

I am amazing.

I am completely amazing and awesome, and I can prove it.

Now let me say something about you: You are more *awesome* and *wonderful* that you know.

Can you picture it? The Creator of the universe, who created you, takes a couple of steps back and looks at you and says, "Wow, you are awesome!" He stands in awe of you, His creation.

God created us and now *re-created* us because you are now a new creation in such a way that we provide an accurate reflection of His glory back to Him and onto the world.

I invite you to look in God's mirror to see what He sees. You will look a whole lot like Jesus.

Each one of us is unique, and we were created to provide the most complete mirror image of God on earth. We reflect "Jesus in the mirror."

Identity Formation

Miles McPherson points out that we have two competing mirrors that we look at that affect our identity formation on the inside. There is a right mirror and a wrong mirror to view.

The Right Mirror, God's Word. As a believer in Jesus, you now have an *I AM factor* from God— your individual uniqueness—which positions you alone above all living things to be in relationship with God.[1] You look into your spiritual mirror, God's Word, to see who you are in your born-again spirit, which looks like Jesus—which Miles calls your *I AM factor*.

Your I AM factor is given by God; it reflects the *I AM-ness of God,* your God image.

> *I am fearfully and wonderfully made.* (Ps. 139:14)

> *You have crowned me with glory and honor.* (Ps. 8:5)

Don't let anyone take your crown!

God has given you a new name—a "Christian." That new name reflects your I AM factor, the real you. This new name has many facets which we will discover shortly.

Jesus, the Great I AM, has put His nature in our human spirit, and re-created our *I AM-ness,* the real me.

The result is you will develop a righteousness consciousness of yourself as you *own* the I Am-ness that you see in this spiritual mirror. You will see yourself as a *saint* and not a sinner. A righteousness consciousness is the gold standard you are to pursue.

The Wrong Mirror. The problem is we often have an inaccurate understanding of our new self as a Christian; were not sure what is the 'real me.' Miles calls this inaccurate view our *I AM imposter.*[1]

Your *I AM imposter* is an inaccurate or incomplete understanding of who you are as a Christian. It is a deception, a counterfeit version or knockoff of who God has created you to be.

Isaiah 55:8–9 captures this understanding:

"For my thoughts are not your thoughts, nor are your ways My ways," declares the Lord. "For as the heavens are higher than the earth, so are My ways higher than your ways and My thoughts than your thoughts."

In the natural your thoughts about yourself are not God's thoughts about you. For God's thoughts about you and me are higher than our natural thoughts. You must look into God's spiritual mirror to see who and what God thinks about you—how God created you and sees you.

One way you develop this wrong understanding of yourself as a Christian is when you try to create a *name* for yourself separate from God—trying to create or find your significance, worth, and value, outside of God. Singer Frank Sinatra sang a song, "I Did It My Way". Have you ever tried to create a name for yourself—apart from your relationship with God? How did that turn out?

Mistakes, Labels, and Lies

You are also looking in the wrong mirror when you think your identity is defined by the *mistakes* you've made or the *labels* others have put on you or the *lies* the Enemy has tried to put upon you. Together, these make up our I AM imposter.

Have you ever made a *mistake* like offending someone with your words; yelling at your friend, spouse, or child in anger; doing something disrespectful; or walking out of a relationship. A mistake is an event; it is *not* your identity!

Or perhaps you have believed the *labels* that others have spoken over you: you're just average or inferior, not capable, an addict or a loser.

> A mistake is an event; it is *not* your identity!

Maybe you have believed some of the *lies* the Enemy has whispered in your ear, such as you don't have what it takes; you're not talented or special; you don't measure up.

And then there's the *negative self-talk* that doesn't let God get a Word in edgewise! If you don't silence those competing voices, they'll eventually deafen you. Which voice are you listening to?

A lie, a label, or a mistake can become the basis of the devil's accusation against you. However, when the enemy hears you assert your identity in Christ by rejecting those accusations, he no longer see only you; he sees Jesus.

If you dwell on any of these too long, you begin to believe them and identify with them, and you think of them as your name. When this happens, they create a wrong mental image on the inside. If you're not careful, the wrong image from labels, mistakes, and lies resulting in negative self-talk will become deeply entrenched emotionally in your heart and very difficult to overcome. A name is a powerful thing.

If you think any of these are your identity, you are looking in the wrong mirror. Continuing to look in the wrong mirror will result in you seeing yourself as a sinner, having a *sin consciousness*.

As a Christian, you are *not*

- what your *mistakes* say you are
- the *labels* people put upon you
- the *lies* the Enemy says you are
- who you've *tried to create* yourself to be

> Your actions or wrong thinking do not define your identity in Christ. What God has said about you and provided through Jesus Christ defines your identity.

You are who God says you are—deeply loved, completely forgiven, and highly valued!

What you may have done is not who you are. Your actions or wrong thinking do not define your identity in Christ. What God has said about you and provided through Jesus Christ defines your identity.

Let's Ponder!

What images do you have in your mind of who you are that are the result of looking in the wrong mirror—your mistakes?

Labels from others?

Lies of the Enemy?

A name you've tried to create for yourself?

An Identity You Cannot Lose

Your God-given identity, which is in your born-again spirit, is something that you *cannot lose.* If something can be lost, then it is not your identity.

Too often we base our identity and self-worth on our:

- appearance
- talents and abilities
- smarts
- strength
- career success

But you can lose each one of these. Remember: *if you can lose it, it is not your real identity.*

Your God-given identity is based on *who God says you are* in the Bible, God's spiritual mirror, and not based on your appearance, talents/abilities, smarts, strength, or successes.

You are who God says you are, and you cannot lose it! The caveat is that you must live out the Christian life and ensure that you maintain your identify in Christ. Just as Adam and Eve forfeited their intimate relationship with God, so can you. Don't reject your great salvation resulting in your name being erased out of the Lamb's Book of Life (Rev. 3:5; Heb. 10:26, 29).

You were created to *wear the name* that you have been given—a name that reflects your I AM-ness from your Creator. Rather than make a name for yourself, wear the name that you have been given.

> *I have called you by name; you are Mine!* (Isa. 43:1)

> *I will give him . . . a new name . . . I will write on him the name of My God.* (Rev. 2:17, 3:12)

Notice that God *exclusively* gets to name us, and not we ourselves or others (labels).

You not only bear God's image but you know His voice. Learning to hear the voice of God is key to discovering your destiny and fulfilling your potential. Know your true identity. When you know who you are, it doesn't matter who you are not. Don't focus on what you aren't; focus on what you are.

Is God's voice the *loudest* voice in your life?

That's the question.

If the answer is no, that's the problem.

Chronic noise may be the greatest impediment to your spiritual growth. When your life gets loud, with noise filling every frequency, you lose your sense of being. And when your schedule gets busy, you lose your sense of balance.[2]

Pursue the truth about you which originates from your born-again spirit (which has access to the mind of Christ), and not from your natural mind. God's Word tells you what is true about your born-again spirit.

So where do you see yourself on the continuum below? Place an "X" on the continuum line below.

I AM Factor Continuum

I AM   I AM

Imposter_____Factor

Let's trade in your *I AM imposter* for your true *I AM factor*. Run toward your God-given destiny rather than away from it. Wear the name you have been given.

Let's Ponder!

How do you walk away from your "I AM imposter" so that you wear the name you've been given?

Reverse Engineering

God the Father has given us the name Christian, but the name *Christian* has many sides of our I AM-ness.

There is computer software available that enables you to connect a special camera to your computer and take pictures of a three-dimensional object with the purpose of recreating that object first on the computer screen and then in a 3D printer. This is called *reverse engineering*.

If you had a computer, an appropriate camera, and this reverse engineering software, and you wanted to recreate your favorite bottle of water, you could do so. You would set the bottle in front of the camera and take a picture of it, turn the bottle one degree and take a second picture, and repeat the process until you have a complete picture of the water bottle. The computer software generates a 3-D wire frame image from measurements, and the 3-D image is dimensioned. Finally, you would send the image to the 3D printer to recreate the water bottle out of a clear plastic. You could then pour your favorite beverage or water into the bottle and take a cold refreshing drink to test your re-created water bottle.

In the same way, if you could use a spiritual camera to take a complete picture of your born-again spirit found in the Word, you would see a complete profile of your born-again spirit. As you look into the spiritual mirror of God's Word, you receive revelation of the "wire frame and measurements" to see a snapshot and reflection of what and who you are in Christ. One snapshot would show that you are *righteous* in your born-again spirit. Another snapshot would show that you are *holy* in your born-again spirit, and so on.

In cooperation with the Holy Spirit, you then begin to form, like a 3D printer, that Christ-image in your mind and heart. Each snapshot is a part of the complete profile of your I AM factor, which is how God the Father sees you and has re-created you. As a 3D printer, the Holy Spirit helps you produce and implant a complete masterpiece in our mind and heart—a replica of who you are in your born-again spirit.

In this book, we will be looking at your complete born-again-spirit portrait and will break it into five smaller sub-profiles to help you better understand your born-again spirit. Once you understand each smaller profile, then you can *activate* each truth about your born-again spirit by revelation of the Holy Spirit and faith to help your soul catch up with what has already transpired in your born-again spirit.

From the I *am,* I *have,* and I *can do* declaration above, the five smaller profiles we will study and activate later in this book are your:

- · *I am* accepted profile
- · *I am* secure profile
- · *I am* significant profile
- · the what *I have* profile
- · the what *I can do* profile

Let's now take a closer look at who God says that we are—and look deeper into His mirror—God's Word—to see what God sees.

Let's Internalize and Apply!

1. What is meant by the I AM factor?

_____

_____

_____

2. How does it differ from the I AM imposter?

_____

_____

_____

3. How do you move from the I AM imposter to the I AM factor?

_____

_____

_____

4. Have you ever tried to create a name for yourself—apart from your relationship with God—trying to find significance, worth, and value separate from God? How did that turn out? Who has the exclusive right to give you a name? How should you respond?

_____

_____

_____

_____

5. How can you go from looking in the I AM imposter mirror (your mistakes, labels from others, lies from enemy) and flip the script so that you look more intently at your I AM factor—the real you?

_____

_____

_____

_____

Chapter 2

The Real You

Now may the God of peace Himself sanctify you entirely; and may your spirit and soul and body
be preserved complete, without blame at the coming of our Lord Jesus Christ. (1 Thess. 5:23)

Understanding Spirit, Soul, and Body

The Scripture says that we are a three-part being: spirit, soul, and body.[3]

Spirit—Our innermost part.

Soul—Our mental, emotional part.
Includes: mind, will, emotions, and conscience.
Often called "personality."

Body—Our physical part.

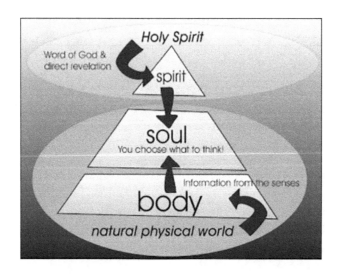

Our *body* has five senses, but those senses cannot directly discern what is in your born-again spirit.

> *That which is born of the flesh is flesh; and that which is born of the Spirit is spirit.* (John 3:6)

Also, your *soul* (mind and emotions) cannot clearly discern what is in your born-again spirit.

God's Word is the only accurate way to perceive what is in your born-again spirit. Looking into God's spiritual mirror is how you discern your born-again spirit.[3] God's Word reveals spiritual reality about your born-again spirit—which is how God sees us as a reflection of Himself. He wants us to see ourselves the same way.

> God's Word is *spirit* and *life. (John 6:63)*

Understanding spirit, soul, and body unlocks the spirit realm so you can experience who you *are,* what you *have, and* what you *can do* in Christ. God's Word perfectly reflects who you are in your born-again spirit.

Each one of us is unique, and we were created to provide the most complete mirror image of God on earth. We see "Jesus in the mirror."

> God's Word is the accurate way to perceive the spirit realm. Looking into God's spiritual mirror is how you access your born-again spirit.

Let's Ponder!

What ways can you use God's mirror, His Word, to see yourself as the Heavenly Father sees you?

Every born-again believer has undergone a complete inner transformation.

> *Therefore if anyone* [you] *is in Christ, he is a new creature* [in your born-again spirit]; *the old things passed away* [from your spirit]; *behold, new things have come* [into your born-again spirit]. *Now all these things* [in your born-again spirit] *are from God* (2 Cor. 5:17–18a, brackets mine)

Your *body* and *soul* were not fully transformed when you were born again. The change occurred in your born-again spirit.[2] The change in your spirit will have an immediate impact on your soul and your body—your whole person—resulting in a changed life.

> *For you have been born again . . . through the living and enduring word of* God (1 Pet. 1:23)

The complete transformation of your body and soul won't be completed until you go to be with Jesus. At that time your soul will be completely transformed (1 Cor. 13:9–10, 12) as well as your body (1 Cor. 15:42–44, 52–53). The key point here is that this transformational change occurred in your born-again spirit and looking into the Word of God, God's spiritual mirror is the only way to perceive your spirit.

Let's Internalize and Apply!

1. What are the three parts of your being?

   _____

   _____

   _____

2. Can you access your spirit in a natural way? Explain.

   _____

   _____

   _____

3. What is the only accurate way to perceive the spiritual realm?

   _____

   _____

   _____

4. What is meant by God's Word being a "spiritual mirror"?

_____

_____

_____

5. What transformation occurred when you were born again?

_____

_____

_____

Chapter 3

Five Truths About Your Born-Again Spirit

Your spirit was instantly and completely transformed when you were born-again. Here are five key truths about your born-again spirit.[3,4]

Truth #1: Everything that Christ has done for you at the cross has already been deposited into your born-again spirit in fullness. You've already "got it!"[5]

Everything that God has done for you has already been deposited into your born-again spirit in abundance. It's there, so draw it out of your spirit and into the physical realm. You simply need the Spirit's revelation of what you already have.

> *For of His fullness we have all received, and grace upon grace.* (John 1:16)

> *For it was the Father's good pleasure for all the fullness to dwell in Him; For in Him all the fullness of Deity* [Father, Son, Holy Spirit] *dwells in bodily form, and in Him you have been made complete.* (Col. 1:19; 2:9–10, brackets mine)

> *seeing that His divine power has granted to us <u>everything</u> pertaining to life and godliness, through the true knowledge of Him who called us by His own glory and excellence.* (2 Pet. 1:3, underline added)

You must see who you are and what you have in the spirit realm through the Word of God and believe it by faith. The Christian life is a process of renewing your mind and learning to release what you've already received in your born-again being.

For example, the fruit of the Spirit was imparted into your spirit in *seed* form when you are *born* of the Spirit. The fruit are planted in your spirit as nine different seeds that are to be watered and cultivated until they grow to maturity in your heart. They are to infiltrate your nature and personality until they become your new nature and way of life. You've already "got it" and simply must activate and release each fruit of the Spirit.

Your Christian life is about learning how to manifest in the physical realm what's already in your born-again spirit. You have the fullness of Christ, but the Lord also *imparts* additional gifts and graces of the Holy Spirit into you for effective ministry and Christian living. You have His fullness in your born-again spirit, so have an *abundance* mentality, and not a *deficit* or deficient mentality.

Let's Ponder!

How difficult is it for you to accept that everything you need has already been imparted into your spirit in abundance?

What does "you've already got it" include?

Truth #2: At this very moment, your born-again spirit is as perfect and complete as it'll ever be throughout all eternity.[3]

You are *perfect* and *complete* in your born-again spirit. Your born-again spirit is sealed to keep out the impurities and evil, and seal in the new nature, which is righteous, holy, perfect, and complete. When you were born again, your spirit was encased—vacuum packed—by the Holy Spirit for preservation. Your born-again spirit retains its original holiness and purity—and will for eternity.

> *For by one offering He has perfected for all time those who are sanctified.*
> *. . . and to the spirits of the righteous made perfect.* (Heb. 10:14, 12:23)

As a Christian, when you sin, that sin cannot enter into your spirit, but it can have a negative impact on your soul and body. Sin, if left unconfessed, can have an oppressive effect on your soul and ultimately on your body. It will also weigh heavily upon your spirit and fellowship with God and with other people.

You will not get a new born-again spirit when you arrive in heaven, and neither will it need to be matured, complete, or cleansed. Your born-again spirit down here is as perfect and complete as it'll ever be throughout all eternity.

Truth #3: Your born-again spirit is—right now—as *perfect, mature,* and *complete* as Jesus Himself.[3]

You are a born-again spirit, you have a soul, and you live in a body. Your born-again spirit is the real you, which is as perfect, mature and complete as Jesus Christ. This should not be surprising because you received the spirit of Christ, God's holy Son, into your spirit when you were born again.

As long as we live on the earth, the temptation to sin will be a challenge. But when the Lord returns and takes us to heaven, then we shall be like Him not only in spirit, but in our soul and body as well.

Truth #4: When God looks at you, He sees your born-again spirit that is as *righteous* and *holy* as Jesus.[3]

> *Lay aside the old self* [the 'I AM imposter'] . . . *be renewed in the spirit of your mind and put on the new self* [the 'I AM factor'], *which in the likeness of has been created in righteous and holiness of the truth."* (Eph. 4:22–24, brackets added)
>
> *He made Him who knew no sin to be sin on our behalf, so that we might become the righteousness of God in Him.* (2 Cor. 5:21)

Let's unpack Ephesians 4:24 a little more: . . . *and put on the new* [not existing before] *self* [*anthropos* = new kind or race of man] *which in the likeness of God had been created* [made out of nothing physical] *in righteousness and holiness . . .*

You are now a member of a new race of people—the *saints* race, or the church race. You are part of a newly created people who did not exist before—a new superior kind of mankind now seated at the right hand of the Father. As a member of the saints race of people, you are superior to the first man, Adam. While Adam was created in innocence, you have been created in *righteousness!* And while Adam had authority and dominion over the earth, you have authority in *both* heaven and earth.

Your mortal body is here on earth, but your born-again spirit is seated with Christ Jesus at the right hand of the Father. It is a *mystery* and a *paradox* that you can be functioning in our natural bodies here on earth while at the same time your spirit is seated and functioning from the right hand of God in heavenly places in Christ.

Unfortunately, you (or should I say *we*) will attempt to bring the old data (wrong self-image, culture, values) from our "old self" over and impose it upon the "new self," and it simply does not work. You must completely put off the old self and reprogram your soul with the "new self" of your born-again spirit.

God's spiritual mirror, His Word, perfectly reflects your born-again spirit, the real you, which is how God the Father sees you.

Truth #5: When you sin, it does not originate from your born-again spirit. Your born-again spirit does *not* participate when you sin.[3]

Your born-again spirit is *not* capable of committing sin. When your *spirit* and *soul agree,* you release and experience the life of God. The Christian life, by design, is intended to be a life of complete *dependence* on the Lord. This is where God wants us to live and walk.

> *Whoever has been born of God does not sin, for His* [Christ's] *seed remains in him; and he cannot sin, because he has been born of God.* (I John 3:9, NKJV)

> *We know that no one who is born of God sins; but He* [Christ] *who was born of God keeps him, and the evil one does not touch him.* (1 John 5:18)

> *As He* [Christ] *is* [now], *so also are we in this world.* (1 John 4:17)

> *For God cannot be tempted by evil, and He Himself* [in your born-again spirit] *does not tempt anyone.* (James 1:13, brackets mine)

However, when you choose to live *independent* of the Lord, your *body and soul agree* (apart from your born-again spirit), which closes the valve of the supernatural flow of life from your spirit; The result is sin. When you give in to temptation and sin, it originates from your flesh (soul + body), and not from your born-again spirit. As a Christian walking in the flesh (a carnal

Christian), you begin to walk like a lost person with your understanding darkened, and you separate yourself from flow of the life of God within you.

When you sin, confess it right away. If you continue to sin, the love of God is not motivating your heart. Continuing to live in sin gives inroads for the devil to work in your life, violates the unity and oneness with the Lord, and will enslave you once again. Thankfully, the Holy Spirit guides you to repent and not to repeat that sin in the future.

When you fail or sin—and we all occasionally do—you may think that God the Father is looking at your sin, but He is really looking at your born-again spirit, the real you that is created in righteousness and holiness.

Again, your born-again spirit is *not* capable of sinning nor does sin originate from your spirit. As Jesus is NOW, so am I in this world—righteous, holy, perfect, and complete. This is not an excuse to sin, but should motivate us to stay pure in your Christian life.

Let's Ponder!

We learned our born-again spirit is not capable of committing sin. How will you change your thinking so you see yourself as God the Father sees the real you?

Your born-again spirit is as righteous, holy, perfect, and compete as Jesus. How difficult is it for you to believe that statement?

How Do You See Yourself?

Respond to this statement:

True or False: "I am a sinner saved by grace."

How you answer this statement tells a great deal about how you see yourself.

If you answer TRUE...

then as a Christian, you still *see yourself* as a *sinner,* having a *sin-consciousness* understanding of who you are. You still have an *inaccurate* understanding of your *I AM-ness.*

If you answer FALSE . . .

then you are *seeing yourself* with a *righteousness-consciousness,* and you are beginning to have an *accurate* understanding of your *I AM-ness.*

We might correct the statement this way so it reflects the way God sees you now:

"I ~~am~~ *was* a sinner saved by grace; *now, I am a saint."*

You now stand on *righteousness-ground,* and no longer on condemnation-ground!

God sees the real you (your born-again spirit) as righteous, holy, perfect, and complete as Jesus; therefore, you should as well.

The goal is to develop a righteousness consciousness where you no longer see yourself as a sinner (with a sin consciousness). Rather, you rightly see yourself as a righteous saint. (The term, "saint," is a very frequent term for Christians in the New Testament.) You honestly and genuinely can say:

"I no longer see myself as a sinner, but as a saint . . . who occasionally sins."

God does not see you as a sin consciousness person; He sees you as having a righteousness consciousness, since that is how He has recreated you. That's the gold standard.

Place an "X" on the 'righteousness consciousness' continuum which best reflects where you see yourself currently.

Righteousness Consciousness Continuum

Sin   Righteousness

Consciousness _____Consciousness

Let's Internalize and Apply!

1. As a Christian, you are a born-again spirit, you have a soul, and you live in a body. So what is the real you?

    _____

    _____

    _____

2. When God the Father looks at me, what does He see?

    _____

    _____

    _____

3. What is the difference between having a *sin-consciousness* and a *righteousness consciousness?* How can you move to having a righteousness consciousness, the gold standard?

    _____

    _____

    _____

4. What does it mean to "wear the name you've been given"?

    _____

    _____

    _____

Chapter 4

The War Is Over and God Is Not Angry

Jesus Christ . . . is the propitiation for our sins; and not only for ours only,
but also for those of the whole world. (1 John 2:1–2)

O ne of the most important snapshots of your born-again spirit that you need to
understand is:

"I am completely forgiven of all my sins—past, present, and future."

From my experience in ministry, this truth is one of the most difficult for so many Christians
to understand and accept as true. You, too, may find it hard to believe and accept that the "war"
between you and God regarding your sins is over, and God is not angry with you. I have found
that once believers understand, believe, and accept this pivotal truth of complete forgiveness,
the other truths are much easier to believe and activate. Therefore, this chapter is devoted to the
subject of your complete forgiveness.

So let's look into God's spiritual mirror of complete forgiveness. This chapter is a somewhat heavy
chapter to read, but it is essential that you understand complete forgiveness to move forward.

First, God has forever settled the sin issue.[4] God is not crediting (applying) sin against anyone.
God has not credited sin to anyone for nearly two thousand years. The sins of the entire world
have been paid for but only benefit you if you repent when you do sin.

If anyone sins, we have an Advocate with the Father, Jesus Christ the righteous; and
He Himself is the propitiation for our sins; and not only for ours only, but also for
those of the whole world. (1 John 2:1–2)

Not only are your sins as a Christian forgiven and paid for, the sins of the lost have been paid for as well. Jesus bore the sins of everyone—not just those He knew would accept Him. People aren't really going to hell because of sin. They're going to hell because they have rejected Jesus' payment for their sins.

If you think God is angry with you and is holding your sins against you, then you'll never have boldness, confidence, or faith. The truth of the matter is God is not angry with you about anything since you have been born again.

Jesus bore the condemnation of every sin ever committed. When Jesus ascended from the grave to sit at the right hand of the Father, there was no sin upon Him because He paid for all sin at the cross. There is no sin upon us either because we are in Him.

You don't want to sin. But when you do, you are not condemned (1 John 2:1 above) since your sins have already been judged and condemned at the cross. When we sin, the Holy Spirit will convict us—not condemn us—to draw us back into unity with the Lord. Let us not grieve the Holy Spirit by not repenting of a sin.

God does not hold a sin against you that Jesus has already paid for. If He did, God would be putting us in double jeopardy for a sin that Jesus already paid for.

Second, you are forgiven of all sin—past, present, and future.[4]
God has forgiven you of all your sin, even sins you have not committed yet. God is no longer angry because you sin![13] Your forgiveness has been provided for and you *appropriate* that forgiveness when you confess a sin or failure.

> *Through His own blood, He entered the holy place once for all, having obtained eternal redemption . . . those who have been called may receive the promise of the eternal inheritance.* (Heb. 9:12c, 15)

> *We have been sanctified* [positionally] *through the offering of the body of Jesus Christ once for all . . . For by one offering He has perfected for all time those who are sanctified* [process]. (Heb. 10:10, 14, brackets mine)

> God does not hold a sin against you that Jesus has already paid for.

To the spirits of righteous men made perfect. (Heb. 12:23)

These verses confirm that you are forgiven of all past, present, and future sins *as you appropriate it.*

The Two-Fold Work of Christ

As you can see in the illustration below, *The Salvation Triangle,*[6] God has justified you based on the two-fold work of Christ. First, Christ rescued you from sin by *redeeming* you. Jesus redeemed you by purchasing you with His own blood. This is what *He did* in relation to you, not what *you do.*

Second, Christ turned aside the Father's wrath forever (called *propitiation*) regarding all of your sins through His sacrificial death. This is what Jesus did for us in relation to the Father. Jesus exhausted the righteous anger, wrath, and fiery indignation against all of your sins (Isa. 53:10–11, 54:9–10). God the Father was fully satisfied with the payment of His Son on the cross and will never be angry with you. When it was completed, Jesus shouted, "It is finished!"

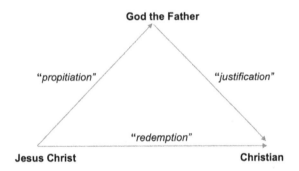

Jesus turned aside God's wrath, anger, and fury against sin through his sacrifice of atonement. Jesus permanently turned aside God's wrath through His sacrificial death. Jesus made a double payment for all sins for all time, taking the full brunt of the punishment you deserved, satisfying God's justice (Isa. 40:2). Now, God is in total peace with you.

In my own life, I've always understood that Jesus redeemed me as a result of His work on the cross, but I did not understand His propitiatory work. When I committed a sin, I wrongly thought that if I did not quickly repent then God would be angry with me. As a result, I was not fully trusting the Father since I was sure that "the other shoe was going to drop" on me because of a sin for which I had not repented. I did not understand that Jesus took the full brunt of the

Father's anger toward my sin and now a sin that I sometimes commit does not separate me from the Lord. Now, God is in total peace with me. The war is over!

The good news is that on the basis of Christ's *redemptive* and *propitiatory* work, God is right in *justifying* you. All of your sins—past, present, and future—have been fully paid.

God's holiness is now on your side. His righteousness is now for you, not against you. You are His beloved in whom He is well pleased because of Jesus' finished work.

Let's Ponder!

What makes it difficult for you to see yourself as your heavenly Father sees you—as righteous, holy, perfect, and complete as you will ever be? Explain.

Do you find it hard to accept the truth that the sins you have committed are already forgiven?

When Jesus died on the cross for your sins, how many of them were in the future at that time?

Third, since you are born again, sin is not an issue and will never be an issue between you and God.[4]

Question: Does this mean that you can just go live in sin?

Absolutely not! How shall you being dead in your relationship to sin return to revive the power of sin in your life? This would be returning to bondage. As a member of the saints race, you have been set free of the power of sin. You do not want to go back and live in sin.

Sin enslaves.

> *When you present yourselves to someone as slaves for obedience, you are slaves to the one whom you obey, either of sin resulting in death, or of obedience resulting in righteousness? (Rom. 6:16)*

Stand firm therefore in the liberty by which Christ has made us free, and do not be entangled again with a yoke of bondage. (Gal. 5:1, NKJV)

Even though you are in Christ, the flesh remains with you. In your born-again spirit, you are dead in your relationship to sin, so do not return to sin and revive it again. Choose to not walk according to the flesh (our old nature) but walk according to the Spirit (in our born-again spirit).

Even so consider yourselves to be dead to sin, but alive to God in Christ Jesus. (Rom. 6:11)

You do not have to sin. To do so is to allow sin to "reign" in your mortal body. If you do, you certainly will not lose your salvation, but you will suffer the consequences of choosing to live *independent* of God. Do not get entangled again with a yoke of bondage to sin. Your born-again spirit desires purity and liberty, that which is holy and righteous, so follow your spirit.

Having these promises, beloved, let us cleanse ourselves from all defilement of flesh and spirit, perfecting holiness in the fear of God. (2 Cor. 7:1)

Sinning violates the unity you have with the Lord and your spiritual oneness with Him.

You have the responsibility to safeguard your body from sin and keep it from being used as an instrument of unrighteousness. Failing to do so would be to *violate the unity* you have with the Lord and your spiritual oneness with Him. Sinning against your own body involves sinning against the one (Jesus) with whom you are united, allowing sin to reign in your mortal body.

> In your born-again spirit, you are dead in your relationship to sin, so do not return to sin and revive it again.

Consider yourselves to be dead to sin, but alive to God in Christ Jesus. Therefore, do not let sin reign in your mortal body so that you obey its lusts. (Rom. 6:11–12)

Has sin died? Of course not. But in Christ, your relationship to sin has died. But when you give in to the temptation to sin as a Christian, you are once again giving sin power in your life. The power of the flesh (soul + body) is strong and alluring, but when it makes its appeal, you don't have to respond. Choose to firmly resist temptation and preserve the unity you have with Jesus.

Sin gives an inroad for Satan to work in your life.

If you go out and live in sin, you're inviting Satan in. You're opening a door for the devil to work in your life.

Sinning is foolish. If you choose to live in sin, you're not smart. But God loves you. God is not holding your sin against you, but you are inviting the devil into your life. You are not going to prosper if you choose to live in sin. You will hinder, handicap, and even stop the blessing because you are not cooperating with God. You are called to freedom:

> *For you were called to freedom, brethren; only do not turn your freedom into an opportunity for the flesh, but through love serve one another.* (Gal. 5:13)

Fourth, God does not impute (hold) sin against you and will not hold future sin against you.[4]

> *Just as David also speaks of the blessing on the man to whom God credits* [imputes] *righteousness apart from works: Blessed are those whose lawless deeds have been forgiven* [past tense]*, and whose sins have been covered* [past tense]*; Blessed is the man whose sin the Lord will not* [future tense] *take into account* [impute sin]*."* (Rom. 4:6–8, brackets mine)

This verse says God "will not" impute (credit) *sin* to you, because He has already imputed *righteousness* to you. When you were born again, all of your sins—past, present, and even future sins—were laid on Jesus. God will never hold sins against you in the future! When you do sin, it is your responsibility is to confess that sin and thank God that this sin has already been forgiven. In so doing, you are not letting affect sin negatively affect your heart, your body, and your relationships.

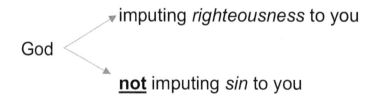

Christ is not profiting you if you fall into religious thinking that says,

"I've been saved by grace, but now that I am a Christian, I need to pray, fast, tithe, study, and attend church in order for God to love me, bless me, use me, and answer my prayers."

You know that God is powerful, but you may think, "How could He ever use His power on my behalf?" This puts you back under a sin-consciousness rather than a *righteous-consciousness*, thinking you have to perform to keep God's favor. You begin to doubt God's willingness to use His ability on your behalf because you feel He is still holding sin against you.

This is religion speaking and not the Bible. Religion puts the focus on what *you* need to do instead of what *Christ* has already done.

Your acceptance is found at the cross because the Father was fully satisfied with Jesus' payment for your sins. Now, your heavenly Father assesses you based on what Jesus has already done. When you do sin, repent and thank Him that this sin is forgiven.

To the *extent* that God the Father is *satisfied* with Jesus' finished work, He is *satisfied with you!*

Question: Is God satisfied with you?

Answer: This is the wrong question. The real question should be: Is the Father satisfied with the cross of Jesus?

Ephesians 1:6 NKJV says you are "accepted in the Beloved," and Romans 15:7 states, "Accept one another, just as Christ also accepted us to the glory of God."

My Doing	His Doing
0%	100%

The original question—is God satisfied with you?—puts the attention on *my doing* when the real issue is on *His doing* based on His finished work. Our adversary deceptively keeps trying to move our attention to the *my doing* column rather than the His *doing* column, putting the attention on self rather than Jesus. We must keep the focus on the right side of the chart, *His doing*. It's about *His* doing, and not *your* doing.

Being and Doing. Your adversary wants you to mix up your *being* with your *doing*. As a Christian, you first must *be* holy in your born-again spirit before you can *live* holy. Because all your sins are completely forgiven based on *His doing*, there is nothing you can add to cause God to love and fully accept you. Be watchful, for your adversary would like for you to think that it was, say, 90 percent *His doing,* and 10 percent *my doing*. No, it has always been *100* percent *His doing*.

In the Introduction of this book, I shared the small group leader asking me, "Are you holy?" In my mind, I was mixing up my *being* holy (1 Pet. 1:16) with my *living* holy (1 Pet. 1:15).

Summary: God placed all your sin upon Jesus. All your sin. Sin is a nonissue with God. He is aware of it and will strongly impress upon you to quit doing it, but not because He's going to reject you. He's already paid for it. God is not ignorant of sin in your life, but it does not change His attitude toward you. He paid for your sin—past, present, and even future sins. When God looks at you, He sees your born-again spirit—which is as eternally righteous and holy as Jesus.

What I may have done (sin, failure) is *not* who I am. My actions or wrong thinking do not define my identity in Christ. What God has said about me and provided through Jesus Christ defines my identity.

> My actions or wrong thinking do not define my identity in Christ. What God has said about me and provided through Jesus Christ defines my identity.

Let's Ponder!

Do you feel that God is imputing or holding a sin against you? If so, are you thinking with a sin consciousness or with a righteousness consciousness?

How can you flip the script to see God imputing righteousness to you?

Fifth, God does not put a timeline on your forgiveness.[4]

Every time you sin, the Lord doesn't have to wait until you repent in order to get that sin under the blood and then be forgiven. Our redemption in Christ was not a short-term redemption—that is, only good until the next time you sin and then have to repent, get the blood reapplied, and be forgiven again.

Truth: Christ entered once in the holy place and obtained for us an *eternal* redemption. God's grace is *cheapened* when you think He has only forgiven you of your sins up to the point you are saved, and after that point, you must depend on your confession of sins to be forgiven. God's forgiveness is not given in *installments*.

If you believe God's forgiveness is given in installments, you won't be able to expect God to protect, provide, and prosper you. It will rob you of your ability to receive God's goodness, blessings, unmerited favor, and success.

This truth about no timeline on forgiveness was very difficult for me to accept for a number of years. I felt that my sins were forgiven up to a point—up to the most recent time that I confessed my sins—but not since that time. I felt He was still holding these latter sins against me. This is what religion had taught me and not the Bible. Religion had put the focus on what *I* needed to do instead of what *Christ* has already done. I was living with a sin consciousness with a pretty strong emotional attachment to that wrong understanding. I was listening to the wrong voice (religion) rather than God's voice that says I am completely forgiven of all my sins—past, present, and future. Now, I have the Spirit's revelation of the completeness of God's forgiveness. I am free to live with a righteousness consciousness in my born-again spirit; I am *completely* forgiven.

> God's forgiveness is not given in *installments*.

So now when I sin, I quickly repent of it out of my love for the Lord and thank Him that this sin has been forgiven on the cross two thousand years ago. I rejoice that my loving heavenly Father forgave me of all my sins and I appropriate that forgiveness when I repent.

Let's Ponder!

Do you put a timeline on God's forgiveness of your sins?

Do you feel that God has only forgiven you up to a point in time?

Moving forward, how can you regularly appropriate God's forgiveness on an ongoing basis?

Sixth, God the Father has given you the *gift of no-condemnation.*

> *Therefore, there is now no condemnation for those who are in Christ Jesus ... Who is the one who condemns?* (Rom. 8:1, 34)

God has given you the *gift of no condemnation!* The more you start (1) to believe that you are righteous in Christ and (2) refuse to accept condemnation for your past mistakes and present temptations, the more you will become set free from hindrances and addictions that bind you.

Even though you fail, there is no condemnation because you are in Christ, and all your sins were washed away by His blood. When God looks at you, He doesn't focus on your failures. God sees you as a learner, not a failure. As Jesus is spotless and without blame, so are you in your born-again spirit—the real you.

Seventh, if you feel condemned, it is not from God. Your own conscience may smite you, and Satan—the accuser of the brethren—may condemn you, but God does not.[4]

> God sees you as a learner, not a failure

> *Therefore, there is now no condemnation for those who are in Christ Jesus ... Who is the one who condemns?* (Rom. 8:1, 34)

When you do something wrong, you will sense a conviction from the Holy Spirit to repent of that sin. However, the feeling of condemnation different—it is an *assault* against your sonship in Christ. That assault is either from Satan or your conscience, but it is not from God. Conviction from the Holy Spirit leads you to repentance and draws you into purity in your fellowship with the Lord; condemnation leads you to despair and hopelessness.

God isn't condemning you (Rom. 8:31–35). Your own heart may condemn you, and you've blamed it on God. *Truth:* God is *not* angry with you. God is not out to "get you." He is not even in a bad mood. God loves you! The Lord is truly now at peace with you!

Remember, God the Father has given you the gift of no condemnation, which gives you the power to overcome your weaknesses and failures.

Condemnation Source #1: Our Enemy

> *No weapon that is formed against you will prosper; And every tongue that accuses you in judgment you will condemn. This is the heritage of the servants of the Lord, And their vindication [righteousness] is from Me, declares the Lord.* (Isa. 54:17, bracket mine)

It is when you know your righteousness is from the Lord, and no weapon formed against you can prosper, that you can now firmly reject every tongue of accusation, judgment, and condemnation that rises against you will fail.

Action Step: Start speaking and maintaining your belief and confession that you are righteous. Use your faith for the most important thing—believing that you are righteous in Jesus by faith.

The enemy pours accusation on you using the *voice of a legalist* to *disqualify* you. The enemy uses the law and commandments to show your failures, to put a *spotlight on how your behavior has disqualified you* from fellowship with God, pointing out how undeserving you are of His acceptance, love, and blessings. He uses the law to heap condemnation upon you and give you a sense of guilt and distance from God. Your enemy knows that the more condemnation and guilt you experience, the more likely you are to feel alienated from God and continue in sin.

However, you should not allow the devil to condemn you for not keeping the Law; for the Law is for the unbeliever and not for the righteous person.

> *But we know that the Law is good, if one uses it lawfully, realizing the fact that law is not made for a righteous person, but for those who are lawless and rebellious, for the ungodly and sinners, for the unholy and profane.* (1 Tim. 1:8–9c)

If you will accept, believe, and rest in your identity in Christ, and live and walk in the Holy Spirit, you will supernaturally keep, and even exceed, the requirements of the Law. Focusing on the law keeps us aware of sin, but focusing on righteousness by grace leads to freedom from condemnation.

The Litmus Test

The voice of accusation and condemnation only works if your adversary can get you to focus on *your* doing rather than *His* doing.

My Doing		His Doing
Self-occupied	vs:	Christ occupied
Self-conscious	vs:	Christ conscious
Me	vs:	my identity in Christ
My doing	vs:	Christ's doing/finished work

God is no shamer or fault-finder. He is no longer angry.

Another Action Step: *Put the spotlight on the finished work of* Christ, who on the cross took your condemnation and qualified you to receive God's acceptance, love, and favor forever.

Receive the gift of no condemnation, as it will give you the power to overcome your weaknesses and failures.

Condemnation Source #2: A conscience not fully transformed to a righteousness consciousness belief system.

Since you are born again, you will need to reprogram your conscience. Your conscience may have been programmed with a wrong belief system from of the old self or religion based on dead works or an evil conscience and needs to be updated.

> *How much more will the blood of Christ . . . cleanse your conscience from dead works to serve the living God.* (Heb. 9:14)

> *Let us draw near with a sincere heart in full assurance of faith, having our hearts sprinkled clean from an evil conscience.* (Heb. 10:22)

Let's look at what these terms mean.

Dead works = the notion that God's acceptance is based on your performance (*my doing*), rather than what Jesus had done with your sins.

Your spirit was cleansed of its sin nature, but you may not have purged your conscience with the truth about what Jesus has done with your sins. Satan is dragging up things you have done. Don't allow your own negative self-talk or the devil's condemnation to destroy your faith and confidence in God because you know you don't deserve His forgiveness and favor. *Reject* the lie that your acceptance by God is based on what you do and *accept* that He accepts you based 100 percent on Jesus' finished work.

Evil conscience = the notion that your core self (your spirit) as a Christian is still sinful; you still have a *sin-consciousness* rather than a *righteousness-consciousness*.

Truth: You have the Gospel—the Good News! God has giving you what you don't deserve—His grace—and He is not angry with you or holding your sin against you. Jesus paid for all of your sins—past, present, and even the ones you haven't committed yet. All of your sins have been forgiven. You are as righteous and holy, perfect and complete as Jesus. You need to embrace a righteousness-consciousness of who you are (see yourself on the right side of the continuum).

Righteousness Consciousness Continuum

Sin   Righteousness

Consciousness _____Consciousness

Let's Ponder!

When you sin, do you ever feel condemned? How should you respond?

What does it mean to have a "righteousness consciousness?"

Eighth, the very moment you were born again, you became as forgiven as you will ever be.[3]

When you go to be with the Lord in heaven, you aren't going to get more cleansed. In your born-again spirit, you are as *perfect* and *holy* as you will ever be. You do have a body and soul that get defiled by sin in this life. Your conscience sometimes reverts back to the beliefs of your *I AM imposter*. However, your spirit is as born again as it will ever be. You are as clean, holy, and pure as Jesus himself in your born-again spirit. You continue to appropriate that forgiveness and live in freedom when you repent of anything that defiles your body and your soul.

> *As He* [Jesus] *is* [now]*, so also are we in this world.* (1 John 4:17, brackets mine)

Let's summarize: Because of the finished work of Christ at Calvary, God has not credited, or imputed, sin against anyone for nearly two thousand years. What God has imputed to you is "everlasting righteousness" (Dan. 9:24). Christ paid for all sins—past, present, and even future for every person for all time. The war is over. God is no longer angry because of your sin. Your sin is no longer an issue with God.

Let's Ponder!

As Jesus is now, so also are you in your born-again spirit. What will you do to internalize and embrace this truth?

Ninth, God has completely qualified us in our standing before Him! He has qualified us for all His blessings through the shed blood of Jesus Christ on the cross, and His burial and resurrection.

> *Giving thanks to the Father, who has qualified us to share in the inheritance of the saints in Light.* (Col. 1:12)

You are fully qualified to share in the full inheritance that is yours.

Don't fall into the trap of looking at your life, imperfections, and failings, and start to disqualify yourself from receiving God's blessings and favor. You may be tempted to think,

"Why would God bless me? Look at what I've done. I am so undeserving."

Instead of having faith to believe God for breakthroughs, you may feel too condemned to be able to believe in God's goodness and receive what He has already provided when He qualified you.

All your *disqualifications* exist in the *natural* realm. You live and operate in the supernatural (spiritual) realm where God has *qualified* you with His favor. God has fully qualified you in your born-again spirit.

Say out loud: "I am fully qualified to share in His inheritance."

Let's Ponder!

What are some of the ways you disqualify yourself from God's blessings?

How can you flip the script and walk in the truth that you are fully qualified in the eyes of your heavenly Father?

Let's Internalize and Apply!

1. God the Father has given you the "gift of no condemnation." What does this mean?

   _____

   _____

2. Are the sins I commit an issue for God the Father? Why or why not?

   _____

   _____

3. When you were born again, how many of your sins were forgiven? Today, how many of your sins are forgiven? Which of your sins today are unforgiven?

   _____

   _____

4. Does God put a timeline on His forgiveness of your sins?

_____

_____

5. If you die as a Christian with unconfessed sin, do you go to heaven or hell?

_____

_____

6. When you feel condemned, what is/are the source(s)?

_____

_____

7. What are dead works? How do you cleanse your conscience of "dead works"?

_____

_____

8. What is meant by an "evil conscience"? What is the remedy for an evil conscience?

_____

_____

9. Will your born-again spirit be further "cleansed" when you get to heaven?

_____

_____

Chapter 5

As Jesus Is Now, So Are You in This World!

As He is [now], so also are we [in our born-again spirit] in this world.
(1 John 4:17, brackets mine)

As Jesus Christ is *now,* so are you in your born-again spirit. Let that sink in. Your born-again spirit is—right now—as *perfect, mature,* and *complete* as Jesus Himself. Your born-again spirit is as perfect and complete as it'll ever be throughout all eternity. When God looks at you, He sees your born-again spirit that is as righteous and holy as Jesus.

To begin to see what has transpired in your born-again spirit, let take a look at some of the truths about you. (We will look at your complete profile in Section 3.)

As Jesus Christ is Now. . .	So Am I in my Born-Again Spirit
To the extent that Jesus is *righteous. . .*	I am *righteous* (Eph. 4:24; II Cor. 5:21)
To the extent that Jesus is *holy. . .*	I am *holy* (Eph. 4:24; I Cor. 3:17)
To the extent that Jesus is *totally accepted* by His Father. . .	I am *totally accepted* (Rom. 15:7) by my heavenly Father
To the extent that Jesus is *well pleasing* to His Father. . .	I am *well pleasing* my Father (Matt. 3:17; Mark 1:11)
As Jesus now is *perfect, complete, and mature. . .*	I am *perfect, complete, and mature* (Heb. 10:14; 12:23)
As Jesus is *crowned with honor and glory. . .*	I am *crowned with honor and glory* (Heb. 2:7)
To the extent that Jesus was *approved* by His Father. . .	I am *approved* (I Thess. 2:4)
As Jesus was *chosen* by His Father. . .	I am *chosen* (Col. 3:12; I Peter 2:9)

Remember, we are looking at how God our heavenly Father is looking at you. When the Father looks at you in your born-again spirit, He sees Jesus. The more you learn about who you are in your born-again spirit, the more you will discover about Jesus. Conversely, the more you learn about Jesus, the more you will discover about who you are in your spirit.

Let's Ponder!

From the list above, what are three statements you can tell yourself when you need to flip the script in your mind and remind self of who God says you are?

We will now look at how you can use the activating process to bring what has transpired in your born-again spirit a reality in your heart and life.

Section 2

The Activating Process

In the general sense, *activation* is the spiritual process of taking what is in the spiritual realm and bringing it into the natural so that it becomes active and operational in your life. In this current study, activation is the process of bringing what is in your born-again spirit over into your soul—mind, will, and emotions and into your life.

> *Stir up* [or activate] *the gift of God which is within you.* (2 Tim. 1:6, brackets mine)

> *Do not neglect* [or do not fail to activate] *the gift that is in you.* (1 Timothy 4:14, brackets mine)

The four steps identified in Romans 10:8–10 to activate the new birth (described in chapter 8) are the same steps to activate other important spiritual experiences of your life. The steps are the same, but the context and applications are different. This is how the kingdom of God operates.

The concept of *activation* applies in every major key area of the Christian life. The activation spectrum is:

ACTIVATION
- to become born-again
- **to develop a righteousness consciousness**
- to manifest the fruit of the Spirit
- to receive the baptism in the Holy Spirit
- to manifest gifts of the Spirit

In this book, we are looking at the second application—developing a righteousness consciousness—the gold standard—where you activate what has already transpired in your born-again spirit into your soul and the rest of your life.

As you may have experienced, what is true about you in the spiritual realm does *not* automatically become active and operational in your life; these truths must be activated. The natural needs to catch up with what has already transpired and was provided in the Spirit. Remember, the end goal of activating what has transpired in your born-again spirit is to develop a righteousness consciousness in your mind and heart. This is how you are conformed to the image of Christ in your inner man (Rom. 8:29).

Chapter 6

The Activating Valve

Picture a target consisting of three circles inside each other.

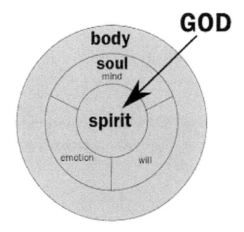

The outer circle is your *body*. It's the part you can see and feel.

The inner circle is your *soul*. It can't be seen but can be felt. Also, it touches both your body and your spirit.

The innermost circle is your *spirit*. Although it's the center of who you are, it can't be seen or felt. It's completely surrounded by your soul.

As we learned in chapter 2, your spirit has no direct access to your physical body.

Everything that comes out from your spirit to your body must go through your mental, emotional part. Your spirit is the core of your being, the real you, your life-giving part.

Your soul acts as a valve[3] in between your spirit and your body.

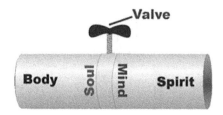

The flow of God's supernatural life from your spirit to your body (natural realm) depends on how open your soul is.

After being born again, the rest of your Christian life consists simply of *renewing* your mind (from God's spiritual mirror, His Word) and *releasing* what is in your born-again spirit.[2]

As you renew your mind and believe God's Word, your soul will start to agree with what's already transpired in your spirit.

When your *spirit* and *soul agree,* you release and experience the life of God. What's in your born-again spirit must *flow through* your soul in order to get out to your body and into the rest of your life. This is being spiritually minded.

However, when your *body* and *soul agree,* you cut off the supernatural flow of life from your spirit. This is being carnally minded.

Many Christians are dominated by what they can see, taste, hear, smell, and feel instead of God's Word. The flow of life within stays turned off because they don't believe anything they can't see. They don't understand the change that happened in their born-again spirit or who they are in Christ. To them, something's just not real if it can't be perceived through their five natural senses.

The Christian life isn't a process of "getting from God"; it's a process of renewing your mind to perceive and releasing what you've already received. You've already got it.[5] You have a well of living water inside of you—in your born-again spirit. It's time to start taking and drinking of what you have already been given!

It's much easier to release something you've already got than to go get something you don't yet have. Doubt is eliminated once you believe you've already got it.

Don't be conformed to this world, but be transformed by the renewing of your mind.

> *And do not be conformed to this world, but be transformed by the renewing of your mind, so that you may prove what the will of God is [in your born-again spirit], that which is good and acceptable and perfect.* (Rom. 12:2, brackets mine)

Your mind, thoughts, and attitudes determine whether you experience victory and the life of God in your spirit, or the defeat and death of the fallen natural realm.

It is *your* responsibility to renew your mind with the Word—God's spiritual mirror—and implant that truth into your soul and heart resulting in transformation.

God's Word gives you the new values and attitudes you should conform yourself to. As you continually look into the Lord's spiritual mirror, you'll begin to see and experience yourself for who you really are.

Let's Internalize and Apply!

1. As a Christian, you are a born-again spirit, you have a soul, and you live in a body. So what is the real you?

_____

_____

_____

2. When God the Father looks at you, what does He see?

_____

_____

_____

3. Now that you are born again, your life consists of what two tasks?

_____

_____

4. Now that you have a born-again spirit, what is the role of your soul?

_____

_____

5. What does it mean when the scripture says you have "received his fullness"?

_____

_____

6. When you sin (and we all do occasionally), does your born-again spirit participate?

_____

_____

Chapter 7

It's a Balancing Act

For by [God's] *grace you have been saved through* [your] *faith.*
(Eph. 2:8a, brackets added)

Grace and Faith: Activating What God Has Provided

Life is a balancing act. The Christian life is a proper balance of God's grace and our faith.[7] Have you ever wondered what is God's part and what is your part in this relationship?

I have come to learn that *grace* is *God's part* based entirely on the finished work of Christ, and *faith* is *my part* in relationship with Him.[7] Grace and faith work together to bring into manifestation what God has already provided in your born-again spirit. Being clear on this interaction is foundational to understanding the process of activation. Let's take a quick look at both sides of this balancing act.

What Grace Is

Grace is the unearned, undeserved, and unmerited favor of God toward you. It is 100 percent what Jesus provided through His death, burial, resurrection, and seating at the right hand of the Father, and 0 percent of what you provided. It's *His* doing, not *your* doing.

> *For by grace you have been saved through faith; and that not of yourselves, it is the gift of God; not as a result of works, so that no one may boast.* (Eph. 2:8–9)

Grace is something God did *for* you, apart from *you*.

By grace, Jesus died for the sins of the whole world. Prior to and independent of you or anything you could do to earn or deserve it, God provided your salvation and all that you will ever need. When you accept Christ as Savior, all that God provided for you was placed in your born-again spirit. That's unmerited favor!

Faith and Believing

What Faith Is Not

Faith is not something you do that makes God move. God doesn't respond to what we do "in faith" and then move. Faith does not make God do anything.[7]
Religion says, "Faith is God responding to something that I do."

Truth: My faith doesn't move God; He is not stuck and need a push. He is not the one who needs to move. Why? Because He moved nearly two thousand years ago when He sent His Son to die on the cross and give us the fullness of salvation.

God, through Christ, has provided what you will need and placed it into your born-again spirit.

So faith is not something you do to make God do something. The Bible calls this notion of "faith" *works* and *legalism*.

Let's Ponder!

Explain why faith does not move God.

What Faith Is

Faith is simply your positive response to what God has already provided by grace.[7]

If what you are calling "faith" is *not* responding to what God has already done, then it's not true faith. Faith does not try to get God to positively respond to you. True faith is your positive response to what God has already done by grace.

Faith activates what God has already provided by grace.[7]

If you are trying to make God do something new, then it's not true faith. The Christian life isn't waiting for God to do something new; He is waiting for you to respond positively to what He has already done. True faith only receives—reaches out and takes—what God has already done, already provided. It's receiving the benefits of the finished work of Christ and the fullness of the Holy Spirit.

God has placed what you will need in your born-again spirit. For it to manifest, you simply must receive it through faith and *activate* the spiritual process of stirring up the gift that is within you. You don't have to make God give it; you just have to receive in the physical realm what He's already given you in the spiritual realm. Activate what God has already provided by grace.

> God is waiting for you to respond positively to what He has already done.

Many people are asking God to do for them what He has already done. They're pleading with Him to give them what He's already given. Then, after praying this way in unbelief, they wonder why they aren't seeing the answer manifest.

Grace and faith work together to *activate* what God has already provided. You must believe that God has already done it. Then—by faith—reach over into the spirit realm and take *and* activate what's rightfully yours.

Sometimes it is hard to understand that everything God has already provided for you is in the spirit realm because the physical realm does not exactly reflect what's true in the spirit realm. Faith acts as a *bridge* to bring what is true and real in the spiritual world into the physical world. We must provide that bridge. Reach over into the spiritual realm and bring what's already done into physical manifestation.

> Grace and faith work together to *activate* what God has already provided.

49

You may, at times, misunderstand the relationship between grace (God's part) and faith (your part).

Question: Is God satisfied with you? Does He accept you?

Answer: This is the wrong question. The real question should be: Is the Father satisfied with the cross of Jesus? Ephesians 1:6 NKJV says you are "accepted in the Beloved," and Romans 15:7 states "accept one another, just as Christ also accepted us to the glory of God." To the *extent* that God the Father is *satisfied* with and accepts Jesus' finished work, He is *satisfied with you.* In your born-again spirit, it is 100 percent His doing, and 0 percent your doing.

My Doing	His Doing
0%	100%

The original question—Is God satisfied with you?—puts the attention on *my doing* when the real issue is on *His doing* based on His finished work. Our adversary deceptively keeps trying to move our attention to the *my doing* column rather than the *His doing* column, putting the attention on self rather than Jesus. We must keep the focus on the right side of the chart, *His doing.* Now, in your born-again spirit, the Father is 100 percent satisfied with you based on the finished work of Christ.

A few more examples:

Question: Is God pleased with you?

To the extent that God the Father is fully pleased with Jesus' finished work, He is *fully pleased with you!*

Question: Are you holy?

To the extent that Jesus is *holy* in the eyes of His Father, you are holy in the eyes of your heavenly Father in your born-again spirit.

Question: Are you righteous?

To the extent that Jesus is *righteous* in the eyes of His Father, you are righteous in the eyes of your heavenly Father.

To summarize, faith is simply your positive response to what God has already provided by grace. Faith only activates what God has already provided in your born-again spirit by grace.

Let's Ponder!

If the Christian life is not waiting for God to do something, but waiting on you to respond positively to what He has provided, how can you reach out and receive what God has already provided?

Let's Internalize and Apply!

1. What does the Bible mean by God's grace?

_____

_____

_____

2. When I receive God's grace, what has God provided? Where is that provision located?

_____

_____

_____

3. T/F: God's grace is only available to those who accept Jesus Christ as Savior.

4. What is it that faith in God does not do?

_____

_____

_____

5. T/F: Faith is God responding to something that you do.

6. Faith that focuses on my works and actions is called what?

    _____

7. Faith is your positive response to what?

    _____

8. Faith only _____ what God has already provided by grace.

9. T/F: The Christian life is about waiting for God to do something new.

10. T/F: Praying in faith means pleading with God to give or provide an answer to your prayer.

11. What does it mean to activate what God has provided?

    _____

    _____

Chapter 8

The Activating Process

Activating What God Has Appropriated

How do you transition your mind from looking at the wrong image (*I AM imposter*) to looking at your I AM factor image reflected in God's spiritual mirror? How does your soul catch up to what has already transpired in your born-again spirit?

You transform your soul (mind and heart) through the process of activation.

Activation is that spiritual process of making what is in your born-again spirit become active and operational in your life. It is the process of activating what is in your born-again spirit and planting it into your soul—mind, will, and emotions.

What is true about your born-again spirit does *not* automatically become active and operational in your soul; these truths must be activated. Your *soul* needs to catch up with what has already transpired in your born-again spirit.

> *Stir up* [or activate] *the gift of God which is within you.* (2 Tim. 1:6, brackets mine)

> *Do not neglect* [or do not fail to activate] *the gift that is in you.* (1 Tim. 4:14, brackets mine)

What's in your born-again spirit must *flow into* your soul in order to get out to your body and into the rest of your life. Your soul acts as a valve in between your spirit and your body.

> What is true about your born-again spirit does *not* automatically become active and operational in your soul; these truths must be activated.

The flow of God's supernatural life from your spirit to your body (natural realm) depends on how open your soul is. It is *your* responsibility to *form* the image of Christ that's in your born-again spirit into your soul and heart.

Activation turns the valve all the way *open*.

There are four steps (principles) involved in activation; the first three are the preparation and foundation, and the fourth is the actual act of activation.[8]

> *The word* [rhema] *is near you, in your mouth and in your heart—that is the word* [rhema] *of faith which we are preaching, that if you confess with your mouth Jesus as Lord, and believe in your heart that God raised Him from the dead, you will be saved; for with the heart a person believes, resulting in righteousness, and with the mouth he confesses, resulting in salvation* [the activation] *. . . faith comes from hearing, and hearing by the word* [rhema] *of Christ.* (Rom. 10:8–10, 17, brackets mine)

> *Whosoever says . . . and does not doubt in his heart, but believes that what he says is going to happen, it will be granted* [activated to] *him. Therefore, I say to you, all things for which you pray and ask, believe that you have received them, and they will be granted* [activated] *you.* (Mark 11:23–24, brackets mine)

Four Steps of Activation

1. HEARING the Biblical Word of Truth on the Matter

All divine truths about your born-again spirit must be received by faith. Faith comes by **hearing God's word** [*rhema*] of truth (Rom. 10:17). You can then know the truth and the truth makes you free to believe and receive.

> *"The word is near you, in your mouth and in your heart"—that is the word* [rhema] *of faith which we are preaching.* (Rom. 10:8, brackets mine)

The Holy Spirit takes the written *Logos* Word and opens our spiritual eyes so the written word becomes a spoken and living *rhema* word.

What is in your born-again spirit is in *seed form* and must be activated to come to full expression in your soul. Hearing God's voice is a *seed* that you receive by revelation of the Holy Spirit and bring over into the natural realm.

2.   BELIEVING in the Heart

Romans 10:10 declares that "with the heart one believes."

> *Out of the abundance of the heart the mouth speaks.* (Matt. 12:34, NKJV)

> *If you can believe, all things are possible to him who believes.* (Mark 9:23, NKJV)

Faith does not operate out of the head by from the heart. When faith is produced, it will operate only from the heart. From the truth, faith is born or formed in the heart and becomes alive and active.

Faith comes into being when your spirit hears and believes the Word of God on the matter. Romans 10:8a says, "The word [of faith] is . . . in your heart."

Faith only functions within the heart of a person.

People often have an understanding in their heart that is based on religion rather than the Bible. A wrong understanding of your identity that is deeply entrenched emotionally can be difficult to root out and replace with biblical truth.

3.   CONFESSING with the Mouth

Romans 10:10b further states that "with the *mouth* confession is made unto salvation." For faith to work from the heart, the mouth must cooperate by speaking and agreeing. Speaking is a "possessor" of the truth.

Believing it in the heart, but not speaking it out of your mouth, is nonproductive. James 2:26b says, "Faith without works is dead"—meaning it's inactive, not workable, nonproductive, not useful, and worthless. Words from the mouth reveal the *amount* of faith in the heart. Words are faith's measuring stick.

Living, biblical faith cannot fulfill its full function without your mouth speaking it. God's Word regarding your born-again spirit is voice-activated, so call it forth.

When a Christian says, "I believe" in a certain biblical truth," and yet does not practice the scriptural principle, it is not faith, but simply an acknowledgment that the truth is valid.

> *I believed, therefore have I spoken.* (2 Cor. 4:13)

You activate what you believe when you *acknowledge* (speak, out loud) every good thing in your born-again spirit in Christ.

> *Your faith may become effective by the acknowledgment of every good thing which is in you in Christ Jesus.* (Philem. 6, NKJV)

Wake up the Word

There is an interesting story in Mark's gospel of Jesus and the disciples in a boat crossing the Sea of Galilee. Jesus fell asleep in the boat and a fierce storm came on them and the waves were filling the boat with water.

> *Jesus Himself was in the stern, asleep on the cushion; and they woke him and said to Him, "Teacher, do You not care that we are perishing?" And He got up and rebuked the wind and said to the sea, "Hush, be still." And the wind died down and it became perfectly calm.* (Mark 4:38–39)

John 1:1–2 tells us that Jesus is the Word. When the disciples in the sinking boat woke up Jesus, they *woke up the Word*. You, too, are to "wake up the Word." You wake up the Word when you believe and speak the Word to bring the spiritual (in your born-again spirit) over into the physical and "make it your own."

> You activate what you believe when you *acknowledge* (speak out loud) every good thing in your born-again spirit in Christ.

The *"You Saids."* One highly effective way to wake up the Word is to talk about yourself—the real you—the way God sees you and talks about you in His spiritual mirror. "Father, You *said* that I am the righteousness of God in Christ Jesus. *You said* that I am completely forgiven of all my sins." Make it an ongoing practice to believe, speak, and activate all that God has appropriated to you.

4. TAKING ACTION

If you really *believe* something in your heart and are *confessing* it with your mouth, then you must *take actions* that are in alignment with what you saying you believe. Faith without corresponding action is useless (James 2:20).

You can determine how much faith you have by *how much positive action you are taking in agreement* with what is true about your born-again spirit.

Activation becomes complete when your soul—mind, will, and emotions—are in 100 percent agreement and alignment with what has transpired in your born-again spirit. Activation shows up in how you *think, feel,* and *talk* about yourself and in your *habits.* You can picture God's Word being true about you in your mind's eye. Others see it in your *attitudes* and *actions.* You are one step closer toward developing a righteousness conscious, one step closer to being conformed to the image of Christ.

> Activation shows up in how you *think, feel,* and *talk* about yourself and in your *habits.*

Let's Ponder!

What image do you see in the mirror? Which mirror are you looking at—I AM imposter? My God image?

Have you stirred up [activated] the truths in your born-again spirit? Or, have you been neglecting to activate those truths?

What steps will you take for old things—mistakes, labels, lies—to pass away from your born-again spirit and replace them with your full identity in Christ? Commit yourself to activate that spiritual reality in your understanding of yourself.

What are the "you saids" that you are going to believe and speak over your life during the next week? The week after that?

Here's the thing: you are already familiar with the activation process. It's likely you have been practicing the activation process in the wrong direction. You have been looking in the wrong mirror—the I Am imposter mirror—and believing and saying about yourself what your heavenly Father has *not* said is true about you. You may have been activating your mistakes, labels from others, lies from the enemy, and negative self-talk.

Reject those wrong images of yourself and choose to do the activation process in the right direction. By faith, begin to *activate* what God has already placed in your born-again spirit by grace through the finished work of Christ. Choose to activate and positively respond to what God has already provided by grace.

Chapter 9

Don't Get Hung by Your Tongue

The Power of Words

There is tremendous power in words. With the tongue you can either bless or curse, that is, speak life or death.

> *Death and life are in the power of the tongue.* (Prov. 18:21)

> *I have set before you life and death, the blessing and the curse. So choose life in order that you may live, you and your descendants.* (Deut. 30:19)

God's Word regarding your born-again spirit is voice-activated. Words create everything (Heb. 11:3). Words are the parent force. Everything responds to words. So, start speaking the favor God has spoken over you.

It is helpful to think that each spiritual truth about your born-again spirit contains a packet of *positive* spirit and life. *Jesus said, "It is the Spirit who gives life; the flesh profits nothing; the words that I have spoken to you are spirit and are life* (John 6:63). You sense that the fruit of the Spirit is also attached to this packet which often manifests as an emotional feeling such as peace.

Conversely, a curse—a negative label someone spoke over you, a mistake you made that you have named yourself, or a lie from the enemy—also contains a packet of a *negative* spirit and death. A negative emotional feeling will accompany this curse, manifesting as a sense of shame, unworthiness, guilt, or condemnation.

- Have you ever made a *mistake,* like offended someone with your words; or yelled at your friend, spouse, or child in anger; or did something disrespectful; or walked out on a relationship? A mistake is an event; it is not your identity.
- Or perhaps you have believed the *labels* that others have spoken over you: you're just average, or inferior, not capable, an addict, or a loser.
- Maybe you have believed some of the *lies* the enemy has whispered in your ear, such as you don't have what it takes, you're not talented or special, or you don't measure up.

If we dwell on any of these too long, we begin to believe them and identify with them, and we think of them as our name. When this happens, you are looking in the wrong mirror and at the wrong image. A name is a powerful thing.

Whether you know it or not, people's words have had influence in your life.

Maybe you left home cursed and wearing a negative label. You were told,

> "You're a loser! You can't do anything right. You're never going to make it. You're
> not going to amount to anything."

It could have come from a parent, or perhaps a counselor, or a coach, or an ex from a prior relationship who cursed you and your future. There is power in words.

Negative words create a wrong image on the inside regarding who you are. Such negative labels distort the real you and contribute to the I AM imposter mindset. You begin to see yourself as a *victim,* rather than a *victor* in Christ.

The good news is before someone put a curse or negative label on you, God already put His commanded blessing on you.[5] The blessing supersedes, overrides, and reverses the curse.

There is power in a blessing that God has spoken over you. And that blessing is much greater than a curse, but you have to believe it.

However, you can believe a curse too. A curse doesn't have any effect unless you submit to it. Satan curses you. People curse you, trying to put a negative label on you. They say bad things about us all the time. But unless you respond to a curse in fear and believe it, it won't stick.

A curse without cause does not alight. (Prov. 26:2)

A curse doesn't have any power over you unless you believe it, unless you fear it. Fear is nothing but faith in a negative, faith in the wrong thing. You have to empower that curse over you by believing it.

For words of other people to affect you and bring life or death, you have to believe them. Likewise, the favor of God—the blessing He has spoken over you—has to be believed in order for its power to be released. Do you believe in the power of a blessing?

When someone tries to curse you with a negative label, let it go in one ear and out the other. Don't believe it, accept it, or let it land on you.

Let's Ponder!

What are some ways words of others have impacted you positively?

Impacted you negatively?

You have the power to bless your own life and future. But sometimes, you curse your own life and future.

So many people are "hung by their tongue." They're just speaking what they feel, saying,

> "Well, they say it's a downturn in the economy and everybody is getting laid off. I'm sure that if they lay off someone, I'll be one of the first."

By talking that way, you're cursing yourself—putting a negative label on yourself.

> "Well, I can't do anything right. I don't have what it takes. I don't have the education. I have the wrong background. We lived on the wrong side of the tracks."

These are all curses and you're the one empowering them.

If You Say So. Matthew 15:10 tells us that there is something more dangerous than eating something that is bad.

When God hears you speak about your meeting with coworkers as terrible, your car as crappy, your kids as ungrateful, your husband as lazy, your town as small, your house as cramped . . . His response is, *If you say so.* You will experience what you speak.

Likewise, there is power in speaking out something that is good.

At creation, God spoke the world to life. At the incarnation, God spoke Jesus into our world. That tells you something about the impact of words. And it should humble you to know that God has given you the same power of speech. That is part of the privilege of being made in His image. You have great power in your words that can unleash a forceful fury that can create, tear down, build, heal, or hurt.

An interesting story in Matthew 8 shows what I am trying to communicate. A centurion came to Jesus for help because his servant was seriously ill. In verse 13, Jesus said, "Go; it shall be done for you as you have believed." This was Jesus' way of saying the word *Amen,* meaning "let it be so." When you say amen you are saying, "May what I have prayed come to pass." Your goal should be to make bold declarations about who you are that, with raised eyebrows, God would say to you, Amen, let it be so.

It is up to you whether the self-fulfilling prophecies you speak become a delight or a burden. God's response to the way you speak is, If you say so.

Let's Ponder!

How do I speak to myself and others? In what way is my speech positive?

In what ways do I have a hard time controlling my tongue?

Think of an area of your life you tend to complain about or speak negatively of. Every time you are tempted to complain this week, challenge yourself, to find a way to thank God instead.

Unforgiveness and *hatred* also empower the curse and stop the blessing. You are the one empowering the curse when you won't let go of the offense you took because of how someone else treated you. It closes the valve and stops the flow of God's blessing.

You need to start empowering the truth about your born-again spirit by faith and quit fearing the curse. Let's stop fearing what people have said about us and what they have done to us and start walking in the blessing of God!

Let's Ponder!

By your words, are you putting a curse or a negative label on your life?

Your future?

Your family members?

Can you understand how putting a curse or a negative label on yourself undercuts the process of activating in your soul what is in your born-again spirit?

God wants you to break those curses over your life and stop them from working against you. But you have to denounce them and condemn them.

> *No weapon that is formed against you will prosper; and every tongue that accuses you in judgment you will condemn. This is the heritage of the servants of the Lord and their vindication is from Me, declares the Lord. (Isa. 54:17)*

You have to say,

"No longer will this curse dominate me. I'm going to receive the blessing of God!"

Out loud, read this prayer and highlight the words that stand out for you.

Model prayer:

"Father, I repent of empowering these curses by believing what others have said about me. Forgive me for being hurt and offended when You've said so many wonderful things about me. You have blessed me. I am blessed above all people on the face of the earth (Deut. 7:14). I repent of letting these curses, these negative words, dominate me. Right now, I take authority in Christ Jesus, and I speak death to those curses. In the name of Jesus, I say that I am not going to let any curse that anyone has spoken over me—or that I have spoken over myself—to remain. I break them all, in Jesus' name. I can do all things through Christ who strengthens me (Phil. 4:13). You always cause me to triumph in my Lord Jesus Christ (2 Cor. 2:14). I am above only and not beneath. I am the head and not the tail (Deut. 28:13).

I break the curses of doctors, bankers, lawyers, and any other person who has spoken negative things— death words—to me about who I am as a person. I renounce those curses in the name of Jesus and refuse to allow them to dominate me anymore.

Father, I believe what you have said about me. Your blessing is stronger than any curse and, right now, I activate Your blessing by faith. From this time forth, I am blessed of the Lord (Ps. 115:15). The blessing of the Lord makes me rich, and You add no sorrow to it (Prov. 10:22). I am blessed coming in and blessed going out (Deut. 28:6). I'm blessed in my basket and in my storehouse (Deut. 28:5). Thank you that everything I set my hand to is blessed (Deut. 28:8).

I speak the blessing of God over my life, and I break the curse. From this moment forward, the curse in my life has ended, and it's the beginning of the blessing. I declare it by faith in Jesus' name. Amen!

Let's Ponder!

How can you develop a favor-consciousness?

How can you begin to bless your life? Your family? Your future?

Meditation in the Bible involves giving "voice" to the Scripture you are dwelling on.

> *This book of the law shall not depart from your mouth, but you shall meditate* [hagah = to mutter] *on it day and night . . . for then you will make your way prosperous, and then you will have success.* (Joshua 1:8, brackets mine)

> *But his delight is in the law of the Lord, and in His law he meditates* [hagah = to mutter] *day and night.* Ps. 1:2, brackets mine)

"*Hagah*" simply means "to mutter." It means to take God's Word and chew on it, to savor it, to ruminate on it, and speak it.

> *My heart grew hot within me. While I meditated* [hagah], *the fire burned; then I spoke with my tongue.* (Ps. 39:3, NIV, brackets mine)

Meditation does not mean vain repetition, but as you are dwelling on God's Word about who you are, ask the Holy Spirit to give you a fresh revelation of what has transpired in your born-again spirit. Let the Scripture burn with revelation in your heart. And as you speak out of the burning revelation, God anoints the words you speak. Now, you have *power* in your declaration about your identity in Christ.

To meditate essentially means to speak it to yourself. Speak it over and over. Pore over every word and let each one feed and nourish you. In so doing, you will elevate yourself into the presence of the Lord.

You activate what you believe when you acknowledge (speak, out loud) every good thing in your born-again spirit in Christ.

> *Your faith may become effective by the acknowledgment of every good thing which is in you in Christ Jesus.* (Philem. 1:6, NKJV)

To acknowledge every good thing in you means to say every good thing that you *are*, you *have*, and *can do* in Christ.

Let's Ponder!

What truths can you begin to "mutter" to acknowledge every good thing which is in you in Christ Jesus?

What is true about your born-again spirit that you can "mutter" about who you are?

About what you have?

About what you can do?

Let's Internalize and Apply!

1. In our study, what is meant by our words being the "parent force"? How are God's blessings activated?

_____

_____

_____

2. In order for words to have the effect of a curse, what has to happen?

_____

_____

_____

3. What can hinder or stop the flow of God's blessings?

_____

_____

_____

4. What is meant by "meditation" in the Bible?

_____

_____

_____

5. What does it mean to "acknowledge every good thing which is in you [your born-again spirit]"?

_____

_____

_____

Chapter 10

Reaching for the Gold!

But we have this treasure in earthen vessels. (2 Cor. 4:7a)

Treasure in Earthen Vessel

In your born-again spirit, you have this gold "treasure in an earthen vessel."

You are a new kind or superior race of man which in the likeness of God has been created righteous and holy (Eph. 4:24). You are now a member of a new race of people—the *saints* race. You are a newly created person who did not exist before—a new kind of mankind that is—right now—as perfect, mature, and complete as Jesus Himself. As a member of the saints race, you are as perfect and complete as you will ever be throughout all eternity. Everything you'll ever need in your Christian life is already present in abundance in your born-again spirit. You are locked and loaded.

Remember, you are a member of the saints race of people and are superior to the first man, Adam. While Adam was created in innocence, you have been created in righteousness. And while Adam had authority and dominion over the earth, you have authority in *both* heaven and earth.

Our mortal bodies are here on earth, but our born-again spirits are seated with Christ Jesus at the right hand of the Father. We function in our natural bodies here on earth while at the same time our spirits are seated and functioning from the right hand of God in heavenly places in Christ! Your born-again spirit, this treasure in an earthen vessel, is a force to be reckoned with in both heaven and earth.

But, you need to reach into the spiritual realm and bring what is true about your born-again spirit over into the physical realm to achieve the gold standard of a righteousness consciousness.

Your soul (your mind and heart) must catch up with what has already transpired in your born-again spirit. What is true about your born-again spirit does not automatically become active and operational in your soul; these truths must be activated.

Let's Ponder!

What's within you that is a "treasure in your earthen vessel"? Within your spirit?

Within your soul?

The Struggle to Activate Is Real

We have a natural inclination to look in the wrong mirror, which results in wrong thinking and a wrong understanding of our identity. This occurs when a person is dominated by what they can see, taste, hear, smell, and feel instead of God's Word. They don't understand the change that happened in their born-again spirit or who they are in Christ. To them, something's just not "real" if it can't be perceived through their five natural senses. As a result, the flow of life from their born-again spirit stays turned off because they don't believe anything they can't see.

> *For the mind set on the flesh is death, but the mind set on the Spirit is life and peace.* (Rom. 8:6)

When your body and soul (often referred to as the flesh) agree separate from what is in your born-again spirit, you cut off the supernatural flow of life from your spirit. This is called being carnally minded because you are walking like an unbeliever. Your thinking can become dominated by:

- your mistakes
- labels from others
- lies of the enemy
- negative thoughts about yourself
- religion
- your senses

Your understanding becomes darkened, separating you from the life of God within. And this darkened understanding negatively affects you, your relationships, and your fellowship with God.

You need to develop a supernatural inclination to renew your mind and believe God's Word, so that your soul will start to agree with what's has already transpired in your spirit.

When your spirit and soul agree, keeping the flesh at bay, you release and experience the life and peace of God. What's in your born-again spirit can now *flow through* your soul in order to get out to your body and into the rest of your life. You have a well of living water inside of you—in your born-again spirit. It's time to start taking and drinking of what you have already been given. This is being spiritually minded.

Remember, you are a member of the saints race. You are a free son and not a slave of the flesh. You are an heir of God and a joint-heir with Christ. Positionally, you are not in the flesh but in the Spirit. You are to put to death the flesh/carnal mindset by the power of the Holy Spirit. Choose to follow the admonition of Galatians 5:16–18 and Romans 8:14, and *walk* in the Spirit, *live* in the Spirit, and *be led* of the Spirit.

The Christian life is a process of renewing your mind to perceive and releasing what you've already received.

Let's Ponder!

What are two things you can do to set your mind and heart on the spiritual rather than your flesh?

Activation Is a Putting Off and a Putting On

Throughout the Activation process there is a *putting off* and a *putting on.*

Let's revisit Ephesians 4:22–25 once again:

Lay aside the old self . . . and be renewed in the spirit of your mind, and put on the new self which in the likeness of God has been created in righteousness and holiness of the truth. Therefore, laying aside falsehood, speak truth.

There are some important elements here that are a part of the activation process.

Put *off*: Put off or lay aside the false (*pseudos* = lies, imposter, fake) notions of who you are. This means to *renounce* and *reject* them as not who you are. *Actively* renounce and reject, and cut all ties with each false notion. Put them to death. *Root out* entrenched habits such as critical words, being quick to anger, and a tendency to be fearful. If you have a deep-seated wound in your spirit from a prior experience that resulted in a vivid negative memory, you will need to *aggressively* root it out of your memory and replace with the truth about your identity in Christ. This can be especially challenging if there is a strong emotional attachment associated with that memory.

Put off wrong hearing—labels, lies.

Put off wrong believing and attitudes.

Put off wrong speaking—negative self-talk.

Put off wrong habits and practices.

Renew: Actively renew your mind with the truth of who you are in your born-again spirit as found in the Word of God, and implant it in your mind.

Put *on* by Speaking Truth: Speak out loud what is true about you and the life within you. In faith, actively *announce, confess,* and *embrace* out loud the truth about your identity in Christ. This means to *receive* and be fully clothed with a new garment.

> If you have a deep-seated wound in your spirit from a prior experience that resulted in a vivid negative memory, *aggressively* root it out of your memory and replace with the truth about your identity in Christ.

With these elements in mind, proceed now to the next section to intentionally activate what is true in your born-again spirit, renewing your mind, putting off the old, and putting on the new man. It's your responsibility to *form* and plant the new man in your mind and heart. As you employ the activation process, your soul will be transformed into the image of your born-again spirit from glory to glory (2 Cor. 3:18) to the gold standard of a developed righteousness consciousness.

Put on right hearing—based on your true identity in Christ.

Put on right believing and attitudes.

Put on wrong speaking—positive self-talk.

Put on right habits and righteous lifestyle.

Let's Ponder!

What are those things in your mind that you need to reject, renounce, and cut out?

What do you need to "put to death"?

What are some ways that you can form the new man in your mind and heart?

SECTION 3

Activating What's In Your Born-Again Spirit

Developing Your Righteousness Conscious

Growing into Full Personhood

Your soul is catching up with what has transpired in your born-again spirit as you move toward full personhood (a "mature man" in Ephesians 4:13)—from glory to glory. Your mind and heart are being "transformed by the renewing your mind" (Rom. 12:2), and you are conformed to your God-image—the image of Christ. The end goal of the activation process is to move you from a sin-consciousness to developing the gold standard of a righteousness consciousness.

The truth of each statement in the following chapters is organized into daily devotions so that you can systematically activate each truth about your born-again spirit. Each day, review the previous day's statements before moving on to the next statement. Follow the four steps of the activation process to apply each statement.

1. **Hear the Word**. Look up and read out loud the Scriptures associated with each statement and meditate on them in your quiet time. Ask the Holy Spirit to illuminate each Scripture and truth and give you fresh insight of that truth. Hear His voice and in your heart begin to see this truth about you in your mind's eye. View each statement as how God the Father sees you in your born-again spirit, the real you.

2. **Believe the Word**. Begin to *believe* and *accept* each statement and accompanying Scriptures. Make the truth of that statement your own—begin to *own* that statement about you. Really own it. Embrace it with your mind, your heart, and your feelings.

3. **Speak the Word.** Now confess the new statement and truth about your acceptance by the Father. You activate what you believe when you acknowledge—speak out loud—every good thing in your born-again spirit.

4. **Take Corresponding Action (*Do* the Word).** Finally, begin to live out the truth that you are believing and saying. Really own the new truth. Put this new truth into positive action. You will know that you fully embrace it when the new truth becomes the new you.

Activation becomes complete when your soul—mind, will, and emotions—are in 100 percent agreement and alignment with what has transpired in your born-again spirit. Activation shows up in how you *think, feel* and *talk* about yourself, and in your *habits*. You can picture that truth being true about you in your mind's eye. You develop *emotional resilience* in your new identity.[9] Others see it in your *attitudes* and *actions*. You are one step closer to developing a righteousness conscious, one step closer to being conformed to the image of Christ.

This section contains a chapter devoted to each of the three "I am" profiles introduced at the beginning of this book regarding who you are in your born-again spirit.

- "I am Accepted" Profile
- "I am Secure" Profile
- "I am Significant" Profile

Chapter 11

Activating Your "I Am Accepted" Profile

W e each have a need to belong and feel accepted. This is true in our relationships with people but especially true in our relation with our heavenly Father.

The statements in this chapter focus on the portion of your born-again spirit that relate to God's acceptance of you.

I Have Acceptance

Day 1

I am *totally accepted* by and *well pleasing* to God.
Read aloud Romans 15:7; Ephesians 1:6; Matthew 3:17; Mark 1:11

Your acceptance is found at the cross because the Father was fully satisfied with Jesus' payment for your sins. Now, your heavenly Father assesses you based on what Jesus has done.

To the *extent* that God the Father is *satisfied* with Jesus' finished work, He is *satisfied with you*.

Question: Is God satisfied with you?

Answer: This is the wrong question. The real question should be, Is the Father satisfied with the cross of Jesus?

Ephesians 1:6 says you are "accepted in the Beloved," and Romans 15:7 states, "accept one another, just as Christ also accepted us to the glory of God."

My Doing	His Doing
0%	100%

The original question, *Is God satisfied with you?* puts the attention on *my doing* when the real issue is on *His doing* based on His finished work. Our adversary deceptively keeps trying to move our attention to the *my doing* column rather than staying focused on the His *doing column,* putting the attention on self rather than Jesus. We must keep the focus on the right side of the chart, *His doing.*

Another Question: Is God pleased with you?

Notice, once again, the question is pulling you to the *my doing* side of the chart and away from the finished work of Christ, *His doing.*

The real question is: *Is God pleased with Jesus?* In Matthew 3:17, the Father said, "This is My beloved Son, in whom I am well pleased." To the extent that the Father is pleased with Jesus' finished work, He is pleased with you.

Activation prayer:

I believe and declare that, in my born-again spirit, I am totally accepted by my Heavenly Father because Jesus was totally accepted by His Father. My acceptance is complete and permanent. Furthermore, I believe and declare that I am well pleasing to my heavenly Father because Jesus was well pleasing to His Father. The Father was very satisfied with His work of the cross. I choose to embrace the fact that I am totally accepted and fully pleasing to my heavenly Father. I now see myself as totally accepted and fully pleasing to God.

Day 2

I am *righteous* and holy (without blame before Him).
Read aloud Ephesians 4:22–24; 2 Corinthians 5:21; 1 Corinthians 3:17; 1 Peter 2:5, 9

Let's unpack Ephesians 4:22—24: "*Lay aside the old man* [kind, or race] *and be renewed* [come up to a higher level] *in the spirit of your mind, and put on the new* [not existed before] *man* [new kind or race of man] *which in the likeness of God had been created* [made out of nothing physical] *in righteousness and holiness.*"

You are now a member of a new race of people—the *saints* race, or the church race. You are part of a people who never existed before—a new kind of man now seated at the right hand of the Father.

As a member of the saints race of people, you are superior to the first man, Adam. While Adam was created in innocence, you have been created in righteousness. And while Adam had authority and dominion over the earth, you have authority in *both* heaven and earth.

Our mortal bodies are here on earth, but our born-again spirits are seated with Christ Jesus at the right hand of the Father. It is a mystery and a paradox that we can be functioning in our natural bodies here on earth while at the same time our spirits are seated and functioning from the right hand of God in heavenly places in Christ. Your born-again spirit, this treasure in an earthen vessel, is a force to be reckoned with in both heaven and earth.

You are *righteous* and *holy* in your born-again spirit based on the finished work of Christ. The key to remember is you are righteous and holy in your *being* (born-again spirit) *before* you become so in your *doing* (actions). Make sure you don't confuse your *being* with your *doing*.

Righteous means you have right standing with the Father with all the rights, privileges, and benefits of a son. And *holy* means you are pure like God, without sin.

Activation prayer:

I believe and declare that I am both righteous and holy in my born-again spirit based on the complete work of Christ on the cross. To the extent that Jesus was righteous and holy in the eyes of His Father, so I am righteous and holy to God. I reject any image in my mind that shows me to be inferior or unworthy in God's sight. I embrace and see myself as holy and righteous in my spirit. Righteous and holy is who I am regardless of the mistakes I've made, or the labels others have tried to put on me, the lies of the enemy, or my own negative self-talk. Because I see myself as righteous and holy, I am now developing a 'righteousness consciousness' of who I am on the inside.

Day 3

I am *perfect, complete, and mature*.
Read aloud Hebrews 10:14; 12:23

At this very moment, your born-again spirit is as perfect and complete as it'll ever be throughout all eternity. You are perfect and complete in your born-again spirit. Your born-again spirit is—right now—as *perfect, mature,* and *complete* as Jesus Himself.

Activation prayer:

I believe and declare that I am perfect, complete, and mature in my born-again spirit. I am as perfect, complete, and mature as Jesus is. As Jesus is now, *so am I in this world! My born-again spirit is as perfect, complete, and mature right now as it will ever be throughout eternity.*

Day 4

I am *reconciled* to God and *adopted* as His child.
Read aloud Romans 5:11; Ephesians 1:5

As a result of the finished work of Christ, you have a position of being totally reconciled to the Father. Your heavenly Father totally embraces you, wrapping His loving arms around you. There is nothing that stands between you and the loving heavenly Father. You are fully reconciled to the Father based on both the *redemptive* work and the *propitiatory* work of Christ on the cross, and the fiery indignation of the Father toward your sin is totally and completely satisfied.

In fact, Jesus made a double payment for all sins for all time, taking the full brunt of the punishment you deserved, satisfying God's justice (Isa. 40:2). As a result, God has adopted you as His child because He passionately loves you and totally accepts you. When the Father looks at you, He sees Jesus.

Activation prayer:

I believe and declare that in my born-again spirit I am totally reconciled to the Father because Jesus has overwhelming paid for my sins and has removed all barriers between me and my heavenly Father. I declare that I am adopted as a child of the Most High God. Even when I sin, it does not separate me in my relationship with the Father because I am a reconciled, adopted child of God who occasionally sins. When the Father looks at me, He sees Jesus.

Day 5

I am *approved* and *fully qualified* to share in the fullness of His inheritance.
Read aloud 1 Thessalonians 2:4; Colossians 1:12

God has *fully approved* you because He fully approved the finished work of Jesus. To the extent that Jesus was approved, you are approved.

Coupled with that approval, God has *completely qualified* you in your standing before Him! He has qualified you with all His blessings through the shed blood of Jesus Christ on the cross, and His burial and resurrection. He has given you the gift of no condemnation.

All your *disqualifications* exist in the natural realm. You live and operate in the supernatural spiritual realm where God has *qualified* you with His favor. God has fully qualified you in your born-again spirit.

The enemy tries to pour accusations on you using the *voice of a legalist* to *disqualify* you. The enemy uses the law and commandments to show your failures, to put a spotlight on how your behavior has *disqualified* you from fellowship with God, pointing out how undeserving you are of His acceptance, love, and blessings. *Put the spotlight on the finished work of Christ,* who on the cross took your condemnation and qualified you to receive God's acceptance, love, and favor forever.

Activation prayer:

I believe and declare that in my born-again spirit I am fully approved by God based on the finished work of Christ. As a result, I am now fully qualified in my standing before God to experience all of His spiritual blessings in heavenly places in Christ. I live and operate in the spiritual realm where God has qualified me with His favor. I reject all of the accusations of the enemy to disqualify me. Those accusations are an assault against my sonship (personhood) in Christ, and therefore I reject them. I see myself now as fully approved and qualified by God, and the enemy cannot take it from me. My approval and qualification through Christ cannot be taken from me, revoked, or reversed. God has fully approved and qualified me in my born-again spirit

Day 6

I am *chosen* by God, holy and dearly loved.
Read aloud Colossians 3:12; Ephesians 1:4; I Peter 2:9; Jeremiah 1:5

You did not choose God, but He chose you before the foundation of the world. He chose you in Christ to be holy and deeply loved. You are part of the chosen race, a person of God's own possession. You have always been on God's mind. In your born-again spirit, see yourself as He sees you as one *chosen* to be loved.

Activation prayer:

I believe and declare that I am chosen of God before the foundation of the world. Before I was formed in my mother's womb, God knew me. And before I was born, God set me apart for His purpose and appointed me to fulfill a specific destiny that He custom designed. I reject every notion that says God does not have a good plan for my life. I have always been on God's mind. In my born-again spirit, I see myself as He sees me: as one chosen to be loved. I am deeply loved, highly valued, and highly favored.

Day 7

**I am a *new creation* in Christ, a *saint* (a "holy one"),
and a member of a *chosen race*, a *royal priesthood*, a *holy nation*.**
Read aloud 2 Corinthians 5:17–18; Galatians 6:15; Romans 1:7;
Colossians 1:2; 1 Peter 2:9–10; 2 Peter 1:4

In your born-again spirit, you are a *new creation*, a new *chosen race* of people that has never existed before. You are a new kind of people. Your born-again spirit has taken on the divine nature of Christ. You are a saint, a "holy one," the term used most often to refer to Christians. You are royalty in this new race that is holy and righteous and a person God now possesses and lives within. You are no longer a sinner, but a saint—a saint who occasionally sins.

Activation prayer:

I believe and declare that I am a new creation, a chosen member of a new race of people. I declare that I am a saint, a holy one, in whom God has taken up residence. As a new creation, I no longer see myself as a sinner but a saint. I remove the image of a sin-consciousness from my mind and replace it with the image of having a righteousness-consciousness. I now have the divine nature of Jesus Christ inside me.

Day 8

I am a *masterpiece,* who is *fearfully* and *wonderfully made* and *crowned* with *glory* and *honor.*
Read aloud Psalms 139:14; Ephesians 2:10; Hebrews 2:7

Because you are a new creation and a partaker of His divine nature, you are a masterpiece to God. You are a work of art—one of a kind.

You are fearfully (to stand in awe of) and wonderfully made. Not only that, God has crowned you with His glory and honor. So you are *completely amazing* and *awesome* and more *wonderful* that you know.

Picture it: the Creator of the universe, who created you, takes one step back and looks at you and says, "You're awesome." He stands in awe of you, His creation.

When God looks at Himself in a mirror, He sees *you;* He sees God in the mirror.

God created you, and now *re-created* you, so you are now a new creation in such a way that we provide an accurate reflection of His glory back to Him and onto the world.

Activation prayer:

I believe and declare that I am a masterpiece to God. I am awesome and wonderfully made by God, and He put the finishing touch on me by crowning me with His glory and honor. He looks at me every day and says, "You are awesome!" I choose to see myself as my Father sees me—a highly valued masterpiece, one of a kind!

Day 9

I am a *child* of the Most High God.
Read aloud John 1:12; Romans 8:16; Galatians 3:26, 4:6

As a new creation in Christ, who is fearfully and wonderfully made *and* crowned with glory and honor, you are a *child* of the Most High God. What a privilege! As a child or son of God, you have been given *authority* as a believer in Christ Jesus. As a child of God, God has sent the Spirit of His Son into our hearts, crying "Abba, Father!" Because you, as a child of God, are now co-seated with Christ at the right hand of the Father; you now have authority in both heaven and earth.

Activation prayer:

I believe and declare that in my born-again spirit, I am a child of the Most High God. God has sent the Spirit of His Son into my spirit, and now I am His child. As a child of God, I now have the right to exercise authority in both heaven and earth. What a privilege I have. I now see myself as His child, and He is my loving Father, and I have authority to exercise dominion in my world.

Day 10

I am *completely forgiven* of all of my sins—past, present, and future.
Read aloud 1 John 2:1–2; Hebrews 9:12, 15, 10:10, 14

The completeness of forgiveness is covered in chapter 4: The War Is Over, and God Is Not Angry.

Activation prayer:

I believe and declare that in my born-again spirit, I am completely forgiven of all my sins—past, present, and future. Based on the finished work of Christ, God has imputed, or credited, righteousness to me and has not imputed sin. God's forgiveness of my sins is not on a timeline because God does not forgive in installments. Two thousand years ago, Jesus paid for all my sins—once for all time. This is such a freeing way to live.

Day 11

I am *free from condemnation* because Jesus has given me the gift of no-condemnation, and I am now a *joint heir* with Christ, sharing His inheritance with Him.
Read aloud Romans 8:1, 17, 34

I now have been given the gift of no condemnation in my born-again spirit and have been made a joint heir with Christ.

The feeling of condemnation is an *assault* against your sonship in Christ. That assault is either from Satan or your conscience, but it is not from God. Because you are righteous, holy, and free from condemnation in your born-again spirit, you must push back against the charge of condemnation from the Enemy. Do not accept the charge of the Enemy. You are now a joint heir with Christ, and you share in His inheritance, so reject any condemning assault against your sonship. (See chapter 4, learning point 10.)

Activation prayer:

I believe and declare that in my born-again spirit I am free from all condemnation against me. Jesus took the full brunt of the punishment for my sins so that I can live free of condemnation. I keep my eyes on Jesus' finished work for me, and not my own works. I will not accept any accusation or condemnation for sin that Jesus already paid for nearly two thousand years ago. I choose to fully accept the gift of no condemnation and live as a joint heir with Christ and share in His full inheritance.

Day 12

I am *deeply and tenderly loved* by God, and He calls me a *friend* of God.
Read aloud John 3:16, 15:14–15; Jeremiah 31:3

You are a *friend* of God and are deeply and tenderly loved by God. God loves you with an everlasting love, and this love sent Jesus to die on the cross for you. God calls you His friend, and Jesus will make known to you all things that He has heard from His Father.

Activation prayer:

I believe and declare that I am so deeply loved by God that in my born-again spirit. He sees me and calls me His friend. I walk in and bask in God's everlasting love for me. As I am God's friend, Jesus, through the Holy Spirit, makes known to me all that the Father has shared with the Son that pertains to me. Thank you, Jesus, that you view me as Your friend. I likewise see Jesus as my personal Friend!

Day 13

I am *highly favored* and *crowned with favor.*
Read aloud Ephesians 1:6; Luke 1:28; Proverbs 4:9

God the Father has made you a "highly favored" (Greek: *charitoo*) one in His sight. Ephesians 1:6, NKJV, says, "*to the praise of the glory of His grace* [unmerited favor], *by which He made us accepted* [highly favored] *in the Beloved.* God is saying to you what He said to the virgin Mary, "Greetings, highly favored one. I the Lord am with you." In fact, He has honored you by crowning you with His favor.

Just as Noah (Gen. 6:8), David (Acts 7:46), and Joseph (Gen. 39:4) found favor in the sight of God, you have also found favor with God. God has declared that you are His "highly favored one!"

Activation prayer

I believe and declare that in my born-again spirit, I am a highly favored one. You have crowned me with your favor. Now, I live and walk in God's favor, because His favor is for a lifetime (Ps. 30:5). I declare that the favor of God surrounds me as with a shield (Ps. 5:12). I simply believe that I am highly favored! I now stand on favored ground, and no longer do I stand on condemnation ground! I now see myself with a favored consciousness—that inner knowing that I am highly favored! I will not let anyone take my crown of favor.

Day 14

I am *greatly blessed* because I have God's spoken blessing on my head, and therefore I cannot be cursed.
Read aloud Genesis 1:28; Ephesians 1:3; Numbers 23:8, 20; Proverbs 10:6

Before anyone attempts to put a curse or a negative label on you, God put His commanded blessing upon you that cannot be reversed. God has commanded a blessing upon you, and when He blesses, then it cannot be revoked (Num. 23:20). Now God has blessed you with every spiritual blessing found in heavenly places in Christ. God has qualified you to share in the inheritance of the saints. Proverbs 10:6 declares that the blessings of God are on your head.

Activation prayer:

I believe and declare that God has spoken His commanded blessing upon me from the very beginning, and that blessing cannot be reversed. I declare that in my born-again spirit I possess God's commanded blessing and every spiritual blessing in heavenly places in Christ Jesus. I now receive the blessing of God, and nothing and no one in the devil's kingdom—including the devil himself—can stop it. God has blessed me, and the enemy cannot reverse it. Therefore, I reject and do not accept any curse or negative label that anyone would attempt to put on me. I now see myself as one who God has permanently blessed, and His spoken blessing is on my head.

Day 15

I am *redeemed* from the curse of the law, *purchased* by God.
Read aloud Galatians 3:13; 1 Peter 1:18–19; Acts 20:28; 1 Corinthians 6:19–20; Deuteronomy 28:8

Jesus purchased your redemption from the curse of the law, as He paid for all your sins. Based on Jesus' redemptive work on the cross, I am brought back in full relationship to the Father. (Refer to the *Salvation Triangle* in Chapter 4.) You were redeemed by the precious blood of Christ. You are no longer cursed but *blessed*. Before anyone tries to put a spoken curse on you, remember that God has put His commanded blessing on you. And that commanded blessing cannot be reversed or revoked.

Activation prayer:

I believe and declare that I am completely redeemed from the curse of the law because Jesus paid for that penalty on the cross. I am now redeemed by the blood of Christ. God's commanded blessing on me is permanent, and cannot be reversed or revoked. I see my born-again spirit as completely redeemed and God's commanded blessing is on me forever.

Day 16

I am sanctified (positionally) as holy to God.
Read aloud Hebrews 2:11,10:10; 1 Corinthians 6:11; 1 John 5:18

You were sanctified (set apart) *positionally* in your born-again spirit when you accepted Christ as Savior, which placed you into the body of Christ. The Holy Spirit is the baptizer, and the element we are baptized into is the body of Christ. This occurred at conversion.

Now that you are positionally sanctified because you are born of God, your born-again spirit is holy and cannot and does not sin. You are now born of God, and the evil one does not touch you.

[Note: The sanctifying work of the Holy Spirit is also a *process* (Heb. 2:11, 10:14; 1 Pet. 1:2), which is on-going from the time of conversion until you go to be with the Lord. This is the work of the Holy Spirit to conform our life to the image of Jesus Christ (Rom. 8:29). The Activation process, the subject of this book, is a large part of that sanctifying process.]

Activation prayer:

I believe and declare that I am positionally sanctified and set part to God in my born-again spirit. I am now set apart as holy to God. My born-again spirit is conformed to the image of Christ and being applied in my mind and my heart. In my mind's eye, I now see myself as holy and set apart, not only in my spirit, but also in my soul and my body as well. As one who is born again and sanctified unto God, I believe and declare that "I am born of God, and the evil one does not touch me!"

Chapter 12

Activating Your "I Am Secure" Profile

We each have a need to know and feel secure. Our heavenly Father has you securely in His hand. You belong to Him, and He is strong enough to protect and shield you. He wants you to know that you are secure in your relationship with Him.

The statements in this chapter focus on the portion of your born-again spirit that relate to your security in God.

To activate the truth in each statement, select a daily devotion to focus on each day and follow the four action steps described at the beginning of Section 3.

My Life has Security

Day 17

I am *hidden with Christ* in God.
Read aloud Colossians 3:3; John 10:28–29

Your life is hidden with Christ in God, which means you have two layers of protection. First, picture one set of hands around you—the protective hands of the Lord Jesus Christ. Outside of those hands, there are the protective hands of your heavenly Father. Picture both sets of hands hiding you, concealing you, and protecting you. Your hiding place and protection is found in both Jesus and your heavenly Father.

You are so protected that Jesus said that when He gave you eternal life (a born-again spirit), that no one can snatch you out of His hand. He further said no one is able to snatch you out of the Father's hand either. You are safely placed and hidden in Christ.

Activation prayer;

I believe and declare that, in my born-again spirit, my life is safely hid in Christ. I picture two sets of protective hands around and about me: the protective hands of the Lord Jesus Christ and the protective, concealing hands of the Father. Because my born-again spirit is safely hidden in Christ and in God, there is no person or devil that can snatch me out of the hands of Jesus Christ or the Father. I am well hidden and protected in God!

Day 18

I am *born again* and the evil one cannot touch me.
Read aloud 1 John 5:18

What an assurance of your security in Christ. Because you are born again, you are now a force to be reckoned with! You are positionally set apart to God with a spirit that is holy that cannot sin. Because you are now born of God, the evil one cannot touch your born-again spirit.

Activation prayer:

I believe and declare that I have a born-again spirit that is holy and without sin. My born-again spirit places and positions me in a secure place in Christ. From that secure position of being seated with Christ in heavenly places, I declare that because I am born again; the evil one cannot touch me or anything that is mine. My born-again spirit and my life are divinely protected from the evil one. I believe, declare, and activate that the evil one cannot touch me! I have divine protection from the evil one. I put on the whole armor of God that I may be able to further protect my entire life (Eph. 6:13–17).

Day 19

I am a *temple* in which God dwells, a *living stone,* being built up in Christ as a spiritual house.
Read aloud 1 Corinthians 3:16–17; 1 Peter 2:5

Your born-again spirit is the dwelling place of the Spirit. The Lord has declared that you are a holy temple, a spiritual house, your temple where Christ Jesus lives and has permanence, indicating you are a place of divine security. As this truth is being activated in your soul, He is building a spiritual house with living stones upon the foundation of your temple.

Activation prayer:

I believe and declare that my born-again spirit is not a temporary tabernacle but a permanent temple in which God dwells. The spiritual house within me is a holy dwelling place full of the life of God.

Day 20

I am *united* to the Lord, one spirit with Him.
Read aloud 1 Corinthians 6:17; Romans 6:5

You are tightly united to the Lord and one spirit with Him in your born-again spirit. Know that in your born-again spirit you are dead to sin, but alive to God in Christ Jesus.

You have the responsibility to safeguard your body from sin and keep it from being used as an instrument of unrighteousness. Failing to do so would be to *violate the unity* you have with the Lord and your spiritual oneness with Him. Sinning *violates the unity* you have with the Lord and your spiritual oneness with Him.

Sinning against your own body involves sinning against the One with whom you are united, allowing sin to reign in your mortal body.

Activation prayer:

I believe and declare that I am tightly united to the Lord and one spirit with Him in my born-again spirit. I declare that in my spirit I am dead to sin but very alive to God because of the unity and one-ness I have in Him. I declare that I will guard my life so that I do not violate the unity and spiritual oneness I have with the Lord. I will cherish that unity I have with my Lord Jesus and do not want to violate it in any way.

Day 21

I am *firmly rooted* and built up in Christ.
Read aloud Colossians 2:7

You have already been firmly rooted in Christ Jesus. Being firmly rooted and established in Christ in your born-again spirit is a finished work. It is a done deal. You are secure in Christ because you are deeply and firmly rooted, and His root in you is not shallow. Christ is firmly rooted in your spirit.

Now, the purpose of your Christian journey is allowing Jesus Christ to build you up in Him in the way He chooses. He is the Potter, and you are the clay. Allow the Holy Spirit to form you and shape you in the way He chooses to build your inner character to conform to the image of Christ. Be diligent to activate all the truths about your born-again spirit.

Activation prayer:

I believe and declare that Jesus Christ has been firmly established me in my born-again spirit. I see myself now as very secure in Christ knowing that He will not leave me or forsake me. Because He is deeply rooted in me, and I am deeply rooted in Him, no one is able to snatch me out of the hands of Jesus Christ. Nor is anyone able to snatch me out of the hands of my heavenly Father. I am daily being established in my faith in Him with a heart full of gratitude.

Day 22

I am so secure that I *cannot be separated* from the love of God.
Read aloud Romans 8:31–39, especially 35 and 39

It is impossible for you to be separated from the love of God! Nothing and no one can separate you from the love of the Father. God the Father cannot and will not separate you from His love. He did not spare His own Son but delivered Him up on the cross for you.

Likewise, Jesus justified you when He died and was raised from the dead to the right hand of the Father where He prays for you. So no one and nothing can ever separate you from the Father's love. Because you cannot be separated from the love of the Father, in your born-again spirit you are an *overwhelming conqueror* through Christ who loves you.

Activation prayer:

I believe and declare that I cannot be separated from the love of my Father. Both my heavenly Father and my Lord Jesus have done everything so that I will never be separated from their love for me. In my mind's eye, I see myself as surrounded by the loving hands of Jesus, and His hands surround by the hands of my loving Heavenly Father. I declare that no one and nothing can ever separate me from the Father's love!

Day 23

I am *established* and *sealed* by God.
Read aloud 2 Corinthians 1:21–22

Being sealed by God indicates *ownership* of your life, and it *preserves* you by sealing in your new nature and sealing out contamination. Your born-again spirit is sealed to keep out the impurities and evil and seal in the new nature, which is righteous, holy, perfect, and complete. Sin and its effects cannot enter into your spirit. Your born-again spirit retains its original holiness and purity—and will for eternity. As long as this seal remains unbroken, you are preserved blameless in spirit, soul, and body. That seal firmly establishes you in God. Your relationship and foundation in Him is sure and solid.

Activation prayer:

I believe and declare that I am established and sealed by God in my born-again spirit. I declare that I securely belong to Christ and God's seal upon my spirit ensures ("seals in") my new nature that is righteous, holy, perfect, blameless, and complete. I have an unshakable confidence in my security in God. I am locked in with God. Because I am sealed and established, there is no one who can snatch me out of the hands of Jesus, and there is no one who can snatch me out of the hands of my loving heavenly Father.

Day 24

I am fully *assured* that all things are working together for good, and *confident* that the *good work* God has begun in me *will be completed.*
Read aloud Romans 8:28–29; Philippians 1:6; Hebrews 2:11, 10:14; 1 Peter 1:2

Because of the security that you have in Christ, you have the *assurance* that God is working everything together to conform your soul (inner person) to the image of Jesus Christ. This assurance was placed in your born-again spirit at salvation. As with any other truth about your born-again spirit, you must believe that this assurance is present in you. This imparted assurance includes the confidence that the good work that God began in you will be taken to completion. This assurance is in your born-again spirit in seed form, and when activated, it becomes fully alive in your mind and heart and yields a confident steadfastness.

God working everything together for us is the sanctifying work of the Holy Spirit, which is ongoing from the time of conversion until you go to be with the Lord. This is the work of the Holy Spirit to conform our life to the image of Jesus Christ. You can have great assurance that God will bring the conforming work to completion.

Activation prayer:

I believe and declare that I have assurance in my born-again spirit that the Father, Jesus, and the Holy Spirit are working and coordinating all things in my life for good. I declare that I have the confidence that the good work that God started in my life will be brought to completion, perfection, and maturity. I believe that the Holy Spirit will shepherd the sanctifying process in my life so that my soul is conformed to the image of Christ. I will wholeheartedly embrace that sanctifying process with my mind, will, and emotions.

Day 25

I am *raised* and *seated with Christ* in the heavenly realm and am a *citizen of heaven*
Read aloud Ephesians 2:6,19; Philippians 3:20

Your mortal body is here on earth, but your born-again spirit is seated with Christ Jesus at the right hand of God. It is a mystery and paradox that you can be functioning in your natural body here on earth while at the same time your spirit is seated and functioning from the right hand of God in heavenly places in Christ. As a result, you are a citizen, not of earth, but of heaven.

Just as Jesus was crucified, buried, resurrected, ascended, and seated at the right hand of His Father, you, too, are co-crucified, co-buried, co-resurrected, co-ascended, and co-seated with Jesus Christ at the right hand of the Father. This is the basis of your authority.

Activation prayer:

I believe and declare that I am co-crucified, co-buried, co-resurrected, co-ascended, and co-seated with Jesus Christ at the right hand of the Father. This is my spiritual position in the heavenly places in Christ at the right hand of God. This is my spiritual sphere of operation, my warrior headquarters, and command center. I am now, in my born-again spirit, a citizen of heaven. In my mind's eye, I see my spiritual position as "far above all rule and authority and power and dominion." As Jesus is now, so am I in this world (1 John 4:17).

Day 26

I am an *overcomer* who is the *head* and not the tail, *above only* and not beneath.
Read aloud 1 John 4:4, 5:4–5; Deuteronomy 28:13

You are an overcomer in your born-again spirit because greater is He who is in you than he who is in the world. Because you are born of God, you have the power to overcome the world. The key is to believe that, in the core of your spirit man, you are an overcomer. As an overcomer, see yourself as the head in every situation, and not the tail; see yourself as above only and not beneath. See yourself as God the Father sees you—an overcomer.

In the book of Revelation, there are promised blessings for you if you overcome: Eat of the tree of life in the Paradise of God; eat the hidden manna; receive a white stone with a new name written on it; be given authority over nations; receive a white garment so your name will not be erased from the book of life; He will write His name on you as signifying you are His; and you get to sit with the Father on His throne.

Activation prayer:

I believe and declare that in my born-again spirit, I am an overcomer! I believe and declare that greater is God who is in me than the enemy who is in the world. As an overcomer, I see myself as the head of every situation that affects me, and I choose not to see myself as the tail any longer. I see myself as above, having the upper hand, in every situation and not below. I know my heavenly Father sees me as an overcomer, and I choose to also see myself that same way.

Day 27

I am *strong in the Lord* and in the strength of His might.
Read aloud Ephesians 2:6, 6:10

You are strong—that is, empowered in your born-again spirit. This means you are a *dynamo* because Jesus has imparted His strength and power into your born-again spirit.

Remember, you are *co-seated* with Christ at the right hand of the Father. You are more than able to be strong in your life. Now, the strength that is in you enables you to exercise and exert dominion over every situation that you encounter. You are now a force to overcome immediate resistance.

Activation prayer:

I believe and declare that in my born-again spirit, I am strong in the Lord, a dynamo who contains the strength and power that Jesus has imparted into me. Because I am co-seated with Christ at the right hand of the Father, I possess the strength to exert dominion over every situation I encounter. I am now a force to be reckoned with, and I overcome any immediate resistance. I am strong in the strength of His might!

Chapter 13

Activating Your "I am Significant" Profile

We each have a need to know that our life has meaning and makes a significant contribution and impact on others. Your Heavenly Father wants you to know that your life has great significance. Your life has a purpose, and many of you will feel like you can change the world.

The statements in this chapter focus on the portion of your born-again spirit which relate to the fact that *your life has great significance.* Your life matters and makes an eternal difference.

To activate the truth in each statement, select a daily devotion to focus on each day and follow the four action steps described at the beginning of Section 3.

My Life has Great Significance

Day 28

I am the *salt* and a child of *light* in the world.
Read aloud Matthew 5:13–16; 1 Thessalonians 5:5

Your born-again spirit is characterized by *salt* and *light,* which impacts both your life and the lives of those around you. Your life has great significance. As salt, you flavor and influence the lives of people you interact with each day. The Spirit of Christ in you influences others in a godly way.

As light, you shine and reflect the light of the Holy Spirit to others. You shine brightly in the darkness. You are a child of light, a child of the day. The light you possess in your born-again spirit has a significant effect on the lives of others. The light in you cannot be hidden. Often, Christians grossly underestimate the power of the light of their born-again spirit on those around them. So let your light shine brightly out of your spirit to others so God in heaven is glorified.

Activation prayer:

I believe and declare that I will release the salt and light nature of my born-again spirit into my soul and life. I release and draw out the preserving influence of my born-again spirit to positively impact not only my life but the lives of others. I will live my life before others in a way that will influence and positively impact others with the nature of Christ. I will not hide the light within my spirit, but I release it to others. I choose to let my light shine brightly out of my spirit to others so God in heaven is glorified!

Day 29

I am a *member* of Christ's body and a *coworker* with Him.
Read aloud 1 Corinthians 3:9, 12:13, 27; 2 Corinthians 6:1

In your born-again spirit, you have been placed as an individual member of the body of Christ. You are God's fellow worker, to flow and work together with Him.

The Holy Spirit is not only *in* you but also *with* you. One of the Greek words for "with" is the word *meta*. Meta means "after with," which means the Holy Spirit works with and through you after you are born again. (There is a different Greek word for "with," *para*, when the Holy Spirit is drawing us to Christ for repentance and salvation). As one who is a member of the body of Christ, the Holy Spirit will be *meta* (with) you to minister as God's fellow worker in cooperation with Him and other saints. There is an *after effect* that you are to release and draw out of your born-again spirit.

Activation prayer:

I believe and declare that as a member of the body of Christ and a coworker with Him, I have been fully resourced to have a positive impact on the lives of others. I now draw out of my born-again spirit and release all spiritual resources to minister to others. As such, I declare that the life in my born-again spirit influences me and makes a significant impact in the lives of others.

Day 30

As a branch (channel) of Christ's vine, I am chosen and appointed to bear the fruit of life.
Read aloud John 15:1, 5, 16; Galatians 5:22–23

Your highest calling is to be conformed to the image of Christ in your soul (heart). Your born-again spirit already possesses the nature and image of Christ. The fruit of the Spirit was imparted into your spirit in *seed* form when you were *born* of the Spirit. The fruit are planted in your spirit as nine different *seeds* that are to be watered and cultivated until they grow to maturity in your heart. They are to infiltrate your nature and personality until they become your new nature and way of life.

You are fully resourced to do what God has called you to do. You don't need to ask God to give you the fruit of the Spirit; rather, you already have them resident in your born-again spirit. You've already got the fruit. You simply need to activate them.

Activation prayer:

I believe and declare that I possess the fruit of the Spirit in my born-again spirit. God has appointed me to be a branch and channel of the Christ-fruits. I choose to activate the fruit of the Spirit to flow from my born-again spirit into my heart and all of my life. By faith, I declare and release the fruit of love, joy, peace, patience, kindness, goodness, faithfulness, gentleness, and self-control to flow through me today as a channel of life!

Day 31

I am an *ambassador* of Christ, a *minister* of reconciliation.
Read aloud 2 Corinthians 5:17–20

When you received Jesus Christ as Savior, you were reconciled to God through the finished work of Christ. He imparted His reconciling nature in your born-again spirit to be an ambassador of reconciliation to others. This includes reconciling the unbeliever to God through Christ as well as reconciling one person to another and you to another person. In addition, you have the *word* of reconciliation in your born-again spirit, which contains the substance you are to speak to others to activate reconciliation.

Activation prayer:

I believe and declare that I have the reconciling nature of Christ in my born-again spirit to be an ambassador of reconciliation to others. I declare that I will be sensitive to the leading of my born-again spirit to make sure that I am in right relationship with others, and if not, I will seek reconciliation with him or her. I further declare that I will follow the leading of the Holy Spirit to minister Christ's reconciling nature through me as His ambassador. I am an ambassador of Christ, a minister of reconciliation!

Day 32

I am *an overwhelming conqueror who triumphs in Christ.*
Read aloud Romans 8:31–39, verse 8:37; Deuteronomy 28:13; 2 Corinthians 2:14

No one and nothing can ever separate you from the Father's love. Because you cannot be separated from the love of the Father, in your born-again spirit you are an *overwhelming conqueror* who God leads into triumph in Christ.

Activation prayer:

I believe and declare that I am an overwhelming conqueror in my born-again spirit. I am secure as a conqueror because I cannot be separated from the love of my Father. Both my heavenly Father and my Lord Jesus have done everything so that I will never be separated from their love for me. I declare that no one and nothing can ever separate me from the Father's love. I declare that as a conqueror, I always walk in triumph! In my mind's eye, I see myself as an overwhelming conqueror, the head and not the tail, above and not beneath.

Day 33

I am *called* of God to fulfill my divine destiny as a *king* and *priest* unto God.
Read aloud 2 Timothy 1:9; Revelation 1:6, 5:10

You have a holy calling to fulfill your divine destiny according to His purpose and grace. In your born-again spirit, you have been fully resourced by God to fulfill all that He has called you to do. In your spirit, you have all the spiritual resources (Eph. 1:3) to draw upon and release.

As a *king,* you are to exercise dominion in the marketplace, your profession, and at home. As a godly person, you are to impact all aspects of society for kingdom purposes. God is calling His people to superimpose His kingdom in the business world, politics, the arts and media, athletics, entertainment, medicine, science, and every other area of life.

As a *priest,* you are to apply the spiritual resources of Christ to the needs of the people. Your priestly ministry will often occur inside the local church.

Activation prayer:

I believe and declare that I have a holy calling and destiny that I am to fulfill. I will activate my divine call by reigning and exercising dominion in my sphere of influence—in the marketplace, my profession, and my home. I am the head and not the tail; I am above and not beneath. I declare that I will fulfill my priestly ministry by using the spiritual resources imparted in my born-again spirit to meet the needs of people who God loves. I will fulfill my divine calling!

Endnotes

[1]   Miles McPherson, *God in the Mirror* (Grand Rapids, MI: Baker Publishing Group, 2013), 7–8, 13–32.

[2]   Mark Batterson, *Whisper: How to Hear the Voice of God* (Colorado Springs, CO: Multnomah, 2017), 15.

[3]   Andrew Wommack, *Spirit, Soul, & Body Study Guide* (Colorado Springs, CO: Andrew Wommack Ministries, Inc., 2008a), 1–5; also animated video on Spirit, Soul, and Body at https://youtu.be/MUiIAZTMiBM.

[4]   Andrew Wommack, *The War Is Over: God is Not Mad, So Stop Struggling With Sin and Judgement* (Tulsa, OK: Harrison House Publishers, 2008b), 3–58, 83–90, 139–144.

[5]   Andrew Wommack, *You've Already Got It!* (Tulsa, OK: Harrison House Publishers, 2006), v—vi, 5, 10, 27, 61–72.

[6]   William Lasley, *Romans: Justification by Faith (*3rd Ed.)(Springfield, MO: Global University, 2010), 72.

[7]   Andrew Wommack, *Living in the Balance of Faith and Grace Study* Guide (Colorado Springs: CO: Andrew Wommack Ministries, 2009), 79–86, 93–100, 107.

[8]   Bill Hamon, *Seventy Reasons for Speaking in Tongues* (Shippensburg, PA: Destiny Image Publishers, Inc., 2012), 119–124.

[9]   Ronald Ovitt, *The Five Signs of a Healthy Christian* (Palos Heights, IL: Gilgal Publishing, 2018), 41–47.

Appendix A

Activating "What You Have"

We each have from God more than we know. Your heavenly Father has granted you everything you need pertaining to life and godliness (2 Pet. 1:3). You have what God says you have.

The statements below focus on the portion of your born-again spirit which relate to what you *have* in Christ. To activate the truth in each statement, follow the four activation steps described at the beginning of Section 3.

- I have the "I AMness of God" in me (Gen. 1:26).
- I have *eternal life* (John 3:15–16; 1 John 5:13).
- I have *peace with* and the *peace of* God (Rom. 5:1; 15:33).
- I have the *fullness of the Godhead* (John 1:16; Col. 2:9–10).
- I have my *conscience cleansed* (from dead works and an evil conscience) by the blood of Christ (Heb. 9:14).
- I have the *favor of God surrounding me* like a shield (Ps. 5:12).
- I have the *abundance of grace* [favor] and the *gift of righteousness to reign* in life (Rom. 5:17).
- I have a *commanded blessing* on my life (Gen. 15:6; Gal. 3:29), and His blessings are chasing me down and overtaking me; I have the *spoken blessings of God* on my head (Deut. 28:2, 8; Prov. 10:6).
- I have the *mind of Christ* (1 Cor. 2:16).
- I have been *transferred* into the kingdom of Christ (Col. 1:13).
- I have been *given great and precious promises* of God (2 Pet. 1:14).
- I have *direct access to God* through the Holy Spirit (Eph. 2:18).
- I have *all my needs met* by God according to His glorious riches in Christ Jesus (Phil. 4:19).
- I have *everlasting life and abundant life* (John 6:47, 10:10).

- I have the *victory* through the Lord Jesus Christ and can *overcome the world* (1 Cor. 15:57; 1 John 5:4).
- *I have the Greater One living in me,* because greater is He that is in me than he that is in the world (1 John 4:4).
- I have *authority* as a believer in the Lord Jesus Christ (John 1:12–13).
- I have the fruit of the Spirit (Gal. 5:22–23).

Appendix B

Activating "What You Can Do"

We each can do what the Bible says we can do. Your heavenly Father has given you can-do ability and power to do and obey what He commands us to do.

These statements focus on the portion of your born-again spirit which relate to what you *can do* because Christ lives in you mightily. To activate the truth in each statement, follow the four activation steps described at the beginning of Section 3.

- I can *do all things through Christ* who strengthens me (Phil. 4:13).
- I can *condemn any accusing word spoken against me* because I am righteous (Is. 54:17; Rom. 8:1).
- I can *reign in life* by Christ Jesus (Rom. 5:17).
- I can *approach God* with boldness, freedom, and confidence (Eph. 3:12).
- I can *always triumph* in Christ (2 Cor. 2:14).
- I can *hear God's voice* (John 10:14).

Appendix C

Answers to Internalize & Apply Questions

Chapter 1—God in the Mirror

1. I AM factor: your I AM-ness from God; how the Father made you and sees you.

2. I Am imposter: an inaccurate understanding of who you are as a Christian.

3. Move to I AM factor by reading God's Word to accurately understand who you are in your born-again spirit, and speak it with your mouth.

4. God the Father has the exclusive right to assign a name to me. I should respond by wearing the name that I have been given from my Creator.

Chapter 2—The Real You

1. Spirit, soul, and body

2. No. My flesh (body) or my soul cannot access my human spirit or the spiritual realm.

3. God's Word is the only way to perceive the spirit realm and my human spirit.

4. God's Word perfectly reflects who you are in your born-again spirit.

5. God gave you a new nature (Jesus' nature) in your spirit when you were born again. You are now a new creation.

Chapter 3—Five Truths about Your Born-Again Spirit

1. My born-again spirit is the real me.

2. God sees my born-again spirit that is as righteous, holy, perfect, and complete as Jesus. My born-again spirit is as perfect as it will be in eternity.

3. Sin-consciousness: see self as still a sinner at my core

    Righteousness consciousness: see self (my identify) as righteous, holy, perfect, and complete as Jesus

4. Heart attitude (perspective) of having received the identity of Christ given by our heavenly Father; to put on and wear the name you have been given; my I AM-ness

Chapter 4—The War Is Over and God Is Not Angry

1. God has made you righteous and holy in your born-again spirit. Even though you fail, there is no condemnation because you are in Christ (Rom. 8:1) and your sins were washed away by His blood. When God looks at you, He doesn't focus on your failures. As Jesus is spotless and without blame, so are you in your born-again spirit (the real you).

2. No, not an issue between you and God now. God the Father accepted the full payment of His Son on the cross for all my sins—past, present, and future.

3. All my sins—past, present and future—have been forgiven.

4. No. Jesus was offered one time to pay for all my sins—past, present, and the ones I will commit in the future.

5. Heaven. I am righteous and holy in my born-again spirit, and all my sins have been paid for once and for all.

6. Devil, or a defiled conscience

7. Dead works view: that God loves me and accepts me based on my performance—my doing.

    Your conscience is cleansed from "dead works" when you fully accept that Christ's full payment for your sins is what makes you fully accepted to the Father.

8. Having a sin consciousness, rather than a righteousness consciousness.

9. No, my born-again spirit is as holy, clean, pure, and perfect as Jesus—as it will ever be.

Chapter 6—*The Activating Valve*

1. Your born-again spirit is the real you, the life-giving part of you.

2. God the Father sees your born-again spirit that is as righteous, holy, perfect, and complete as Jesus.

3. *Renewing* my mind and *releasing* by acknowledging every good thing in you in Christ.

4. To agree/cooperate with your born-again spirit to release and experience the life of God; to open the valve to the life of the Spirit.

5. You have the fullness of God in my born-again spirit. As such, God has placed everything you will ever need in your born-again spirit.

6. No, your born-again spirit is not capable of sinning. When you sin, it originates from your flesh (body and soul agreeing), and not from your born-again spirit.

Chapter 7—*It's a Balancing Act*

1. What does the Bible mean by God's grace?

   Grace is the unearned, undeserved, and unmerited favor of God toward me, and is 100 percent what God did for me.

2. When I was born again, God placed everything I would need in my born-again spirit.

3. False: God's grace was made available to all people whether they receive it or not.

4. Faith is not something that makes God move or do anything.

5. False. Again, faith does not make God do anything.

6. Works, legalism

7. To what God has already provided by grace. It is based on the finished work of Christ on the cross.

8. Activates (appropriates is acceptable)

9. False. The Christian life is about you responding positively to what He has already done.

10. False. You don't need to plead with God to give you what He has already given through Christ. It's about believing and releasing. You've already got it.

11. You activate what God has provided by believing and speaking/declaring the promises of God, which are the "'You saids."

Chapter 9—Don't Get Hung by Your Tongue

1. Words have creative power, and spoken words create in the natural realm. Everything responds to words that are believed.

2. Words have the effect of a curse when the words are believed or feared.

3. Unforgiveness and hatred will hinder or stop the flow of God's blessings.

4. Biblical meditation means "to mutter" or speak God's Word to yourself. It means to take God's Word and chew on it, to savor it, to ruminate on it, and to speak it.

5. To acknowledge every good thing in you means to say every good thing that you are, you have, and can do in Christ.

Recommended Reading

Miles McPherson, *God in the Mirror* (Grand Rapids, MI: Baker Publishing Group, 2013).

Andrew Wommack, *Spirit, Soul, & Body Study Guide* (Colorado Springs, CO: Andrew Wommack Ministries, Inc., 2008a); also animated video on Spirit, Soul, and Body at https://youtu.be/MUiIAZTMiBM.

Andrew Wommack, *The War Is Over: God Is Not Mad, So Stop Struggling With Sin and Judgement* (Tulsa, OK: Harrison House Publishers, 2008b).

Andrew Wommack, *You've Already Got It!* (Tulsa, OK: Harrison House Publishers, 2006).

Ronald Ovitt, *Power Up: Emotional Learning Through Scriptures* (Palos Heights, IL: Gilgal Publishing, 2018).

Mark Batterson, *Whisper: How to Hear the Voice of God* (Colorado Springs, CO: Multnomah, 2017).

Joel Osteen, *The Power of I AM* (New York, NY: FaithWorks, 2015).

Michele Cushatt, *I Am* (Grand Rapids, MI: Zondervan, 2017); written to women.

Neil Anderson, *Who I Am in Christ: A Devotional* (Ventura, CA: Regal Books, 2001).

About the Author

Dr. Lon Stettler is an ordained minister and educator who is very passionate about discipleship and maturity. He has been very active in the discipleship ministry for over four decades. Lon has written, preached, and taught discipleship courses for more than thirty years. He holds a doctor of philosophy degree from Miami University in educational leadership and served as a school district administrator for twenty-six years. Lon and his wife, Laurie, have four children and live near Charleston, South Carolina. Contact: lon.stettler@gmail.com